MEDITERRANEAN DIET MASTERY FOR BEGINNERS

2000 DAYS OF BUDGET-FRIENDLY RECIPES FOR A HEALTHY LIFESTYLE | QUICK & NUTRITIOUS 30 - MINUTE MEALS WITH COMPREHENSIVE MEAL PLAN

Maggie Macy

Disclaimer:

The information in Mediterranean Diet Mastery for Beginners is provided for general informational purposes only and is not intended as a substitute for medical advice, diagnosis, or treatment. Always seek the advice of your physician, registered dietitian, or other qualified healthcare providers before starting any new diet, especially if you have any pre-existing medical conditions or dietary restrictions.

While the author has made every effort to ensure that the content of this book is accurate and up to date, neither the author nor the publisher assumes any responsibility for errors, omissions, or contrary interpretations of the subject matter. The recipes and nutritional information provided are intended to serve as a general guide, and individual nutritional needs may vary.

The author and publisher shall not be liable or responsible for any loss, injury, or damage arising from the use of the recipes or information contained in this book. By using this cookbook, you acknowledge that you are responsible for your own dietary decisions and should always consult with a healthcare professional before making significant changes to your diet.

Maggie Macy
2024

Table of Contents

Introduction

BENEFITS OF THE MEDITERRANEAN DIET

The Mediterranean diet has long been celebrated as one of the healthiest dietary plans in the world, revered not just for its culinary appeal but also for its extensive health benefits. This diet, inspired by the traditional eating patterns of the countries bordering the Mediterranean Sea, particularly Greece, Italy, and Spain, offers a sustainable and enjoyable approach to long-term health. Here's a detailed look at how adopting this diet can enhance your well-being:

- Boosts Heart Health: The Mediterranean diet is particularly beneficial for heart health due to its high content of monounsaturated fats from olive oil and omega-3 fatty acids from fish. These fats help reduce the levels of LDL cholesterol (the "bad" cholesterol) and increase HDL cholesterol (the "good" cholesterol), lowering the risk of heart disease significantly.

- Controls Blood Sugar Levels: The Mediterranean diet is beneficial for people with or at risk of type 2 diabetes as it emphasizes low glycemic index foods that help stabilize blood sugar levels. The diet's rich variety of fiber also aids in this regard, preventing sudden spikes and dips in glucose levels.

- Promotes Longevity: Adopting the Mediterranean diet has been associated with increased life expectancy. This is likely due to its ability to help prevent the onset of many chronic diseases and its emphasis on fresh, antioxidant-rich foods.

- Supports Weight Loss and Management: This diet encourages eating various nutrient-dense foods that help manage weight effectively. The high fiber content from fruits, vegetables, and whole grains means meals are satisfying and full without being overly caloric, which naturally helps maintain a healthy weight.

- Enhances Cognitive Function: There is compelling evidence suggesting that the diet's high intake of healthy fats, fruits, vegetables, and nuts can diminish cognitive decline with aging and reduce the risk of developing neurodegenerative diseases like Alzheimer's.

- Reduces Risk of Cancer: The antioxidants and fibers present in the diet's plant-based foods play a crucial role in cancer prevention. These elements help mitigate inflammation and protect against cell damage that could lead to cancer.

- Improves Bone Health: Rich in calcium and vitamin D, the Mediterranean diet aids in maintaining strong and healthy bones. Regular consumption of dairy products, fish, and green leafy vegetables provides the necessary nutrients to help ward off osteoporosis.

- Boosts Mood and Energy Levels: Balancing carbohydrates, proteins, and healthy fats ensures that energy is released slowly throughout the day, which helps maintain steady energy levels and supports overall mood.

Embracing the Mediterranean diet involves simple changes like increasing your intake of vegetables, fruits, whole grains, and healthy fats while enjoying meals with others. Its benefits extend far beyond simple nutrition, offering a wholesome lifestyle choice conducive to overall health and longevity. Whether you're looking to overhaul your eating habits or simply integrate more plant-based foods into your diet, the Mediterranean diet is a delightful and healthful choice.

Interesting Fact: The Mediterranean diet was added to UNESCO's list of Intangible Cultural Heritage of Humanity in 2010.

Success Key
EVERYTHING ABOUT OLIVE OIL

Olive oil, a cornerstone of the Mediterranean diet, is revered not only for its versatility and flavor but also for its numerous health benefits. This essential oil, extracted from the fruit of the olive tree, is a staple in kitchens worldwide, used for cooking, dressings, and even medicinal purposes. Here's a comprehensive guide to understanding olive oil, including some interesting facts and practical tips for choosing the right type.

Extra Virgin Olive Oil (EVOO)
This is the highest quality olive oil, characterized by its perfect flavor, aroma, and higher phenolic content. It is obtained from the first cold pressing of the olives, without the use of chemicals or extreme heat, which preserves the natural taste and benefits of the oil.

Virgin Olive Oil
Like EVOO, this oil is slightly lower in quality but still made via the same process. It has a good flavor but a higher acidity level.

Refined Olive Oil
This oil is created by refining virgin olive oil. The refining process removes flavor, color, and odor, leaving behind a very pure form of olive oil that lacks much of the character of virgin oil.

Pure or Regular Olive Oil
Often simply labeled as "olive oil," this is a blend of refined and virgin olive oils. It is more neutral in flavor and color, suitable for all-purpose cooking but lacking in the nutrients present in higher grades.

Selecting the right olive oil can elevate your cooking, enhance flavors, and contribute to a healthier diet. Here's how you can choose the best olive oil for your kitchen:

- Extra virgin olive oil should have a distinctly fresh and fruity taste with a hint of bitterness. A quality EVOO will leave a peppery sensation in the throat, a natural characteristic of oils rich in polyphenols. These polyphenols are antioxidants that contribute to the oil's health benefits and overall quality. If the oil tastes flat or rancid, it's likely oxidized or of inferior quality.

- Unlike wine, olive oil does not improve with age. Freshness is key to capturing the best flavor and health benefits. Always check the harvest date on the bottle; opt for oil from the current or most recent harvest year. This ensures you are getting an oil that retains its sensory qualities and nutritional properties.
- The origin of olive oil can greatly affect its flavor and quality. Quality oils often list a specific region or country of origin. This detail is important because it indicates a traceable source associated with higher production standards. Avoid oils that only state where they were packed or distributed, as this often masks the true origin and potentially lowers standards of production.
- How olive oil is stored can impact its quality. Light and heat are enemies of olive oil, causing it to degrade faster. Choose olive oil in dark glass bottles, tin containers, or even boxes that protect it from light. Additionally, make sure to store the oil in a cool, dark place in your kitchen to preserve its freshness and flavor.
- To maintain the quality of olive oil, keep it in a cool, dark place away from heat sources like the stove or oven. It's best used within six months to a year of opening but can last up to two years from the bottling date if stored properly.

Understanding these aspects of olive oil will help you make informed choices about buying and using different types of olive oil in your cooking, ensuring that you enjoy all the flavor and health benefits this amazing oil offers.

Interesting Fact: Did you know that the olive tree symbolizes abundance, glory, and peace? Olive branches were historically used to crown the victors of both games and wars, and the olive tree itself can live for hundreds, even thousands, of years, with some trees in the Mediterranean believed to be over 2,000 years old!

Herbs, Spices, and Fresh Flavors

Herbs and spices are the backbone of flavorful cooking, especially in cuisines that prioritize freshness and depth in their dishes, like Mediterranean cooking. Understanding how to use these ingredients can transform your meals from ordinary to extraordinary. Here's a guide to the world of herbs and spices, and how they enhance the culinary experience.

Fresh herbs are best used at the end of cooking or as a garnish to preserve their delicate flavors and vibrant color. They are perfect for salads, dressings, and marinades. For robust dishes that cook longer, such as stews and sauces, dried herbs are more suitable as they release flavors slowly throughout the cooking process.

Spices, on the other hand, often need a bit more finesse. Whole spices, such as cumin seeds, mustard seeds, and cloves, release their full potential when toasted lightly in a dry pan or cooked in oil. This process, known as tempering, awakens the essential oils in the spices and releases flavors that permeate the dish with aromatic depth. Ground spices are wonderful for adding quick flavor but should be used with caution to avoid overpowering dishes.

Breakfast Dishes
Cinnamon, nutmeg, and vanilla are perfect for sweet breakfast items like oatmeal, pancakes, and French toast, providing a warm, comforting flavor. Fresh herbs like chives, parsley, and dill work wonderfully in egg dishes such as omelets and scrambled eggs, adding freshness and color.

Meat Dishes
Rosemary, garlic, and sage are classic with lamb and beef, offering an earthy flavor that complements red meats well.
Smoked paprika, oregano, and thyme are great for chicken and pork, providing a Mediterranean flair that enhances the natural flavors of the meat.

Fish and Seafood

Dill, lemon zest, and tarragon pair beautifully with fish, especially lighter varieties like tilapia and cod, giving a fresh, tangy kick to the dishes. Saffron, garlic, and parsley are ideal for seafood dishes like paella and seafood stews, infusing the food with color and vibrant flavor.

Soups and Stews

Bay leaves, thyme, and rosemary are excellent in hearty stews and broths, lending a robust flavor that deepens with cooking time.
Cumin, coriander, and turmeric add depth and a bit of spice to lentil soups and vegetable stews, creating a rich, complex base.

Vegetarian Dishes

Basil, mint, and cilantro bring freshness to salads, wraps, and vegetarian pizzas, making the dishes pop with each bite.
Cardamom, cloves, and cinnamon are suited for vegetable curries and dishes with a sweet-savory profile, like roasted carrots or squash.

Interesting Fact: Did you know that saffron, often used in Mediterranean and Middle Eastern cuisines, is the most expensive spice in the world? It's derived from the saffron crocus flower, and it takes approximately 75,000 blossoms or 225,000 hand-picked stigmas to make a single pound, which is why it's so prized and costly.

Marinades

Marinades are a crucial tool in any cook's arsenal, offering a simple yet effective method for enhancing the flavor and texture of food, particularly meats and vegetables. Understanding how marinades work, and the key components involved can help transform your everyday dishes into gourmet meals. Here's a breakdown of what goes into a marinade and how each element works to improve your cooking.

Acids: Acids such as vinegar, lemon juice, or yogurt serve to tenderize the protein in meats by breaking down tough fibers. This not only softens the meat but also allows it to better retain moisture during cooking, making it juicier and more flavorful.

Sweeteners: Ingredients like sugar, honey, or molasses can be added to balance the acidity of the marinade. Sweeteners also help in caramelizing the surface of the meat when cooked at high temperatures, creating a desirable crispy, browned exterior.
For the best results, marinate meats for several hours or even overnight. However, delicate proteins like fish should only be marinated for short periods to avoid becoming mushy.

Fats: Oils are a common base in many marinades. Fat helps dissolve fat-soluble flavor compounds in spices and herbs, aiding in their release into the meat. Additionally, fats help keep the meat moist and prevent it from drying out during the cooking process.
Seasonings: This includes a wide range of herbs, spices, and seasonings like salt, pepper, garlic, and onions. Seasonings add depth and complexity to the flavor profile of your marinade. Salt is particularly important as it helps in moisture retention and flavor penetration by breaking down proteins.

Always marinate in the refrigerator to keep the food safe from bacterial growth.
If you plan to use the marinade as a sauce, make sure to boil it first to eliminate any harmful bacteria.

By mastering the art of marinating, you can elevate your culinary creations, adding layers of flavor and ensuring every bite is as delicious as it is tender. Whether you're preparing a quick dinner or a festive meal, a good marinade is an essential recipe in your cooking repertoire.

GARLIC AND ROSEMARY MARINADE FOR BEEF

INGREDIENTS

- 1/3 cup extra virgin olive oil
- 1/4 cup red wine vinegar
- 4 cloves garlic, minced
- 2 tablespoons fresh rosemary, chopped
- 1 tablespoon Dijon mustard
- 1 teaspoon black pepper
- 1/2 teaspoon salt

DIRECTIONS:

1. In a bowl, whisk together the olive oil, red wine vinegar, garlic, rosemary, mustard, pepper, and salt.
2. Place the beef cuts (such as steaks or a roast) in a resealable plastic bag or a shallow dish.
3. Pour the marinade over the beef, ensuring all pieces are well coated.
4. Refrigerate for at least 4 hours or overnight, turning occasionally.
5. Remove the beef from the marinade and cook as desired; discard the used marinade.

Chef's Tip: For a richer flavor, roast the garlic before mincing. Roasted garlic's sweeter taste enriches the marinade beautifully. To lower sodium, replace salt with dried herbs like thyme or oregano, enhancing flavor without adding sodium.

LEMON AND THYME MARINADE FOR CHICKEN

INGREDIENTS

- 1/2 cup extra virgin olive oil
- 1/3 cup fresh lemon juice
- 1/4 cup fresh thyme leaves
- 3 cloves garlic, minced
- 1 teaspoon salt
- 1/2 teaspoon freshly ground black pepper

DIRECTIONS:

1. Mix all ingredients in a bowl to blend well.
2. Put chicken pieces in a sealable bag or marinating dish.
3. Pour marinade over chicken, coating evenly.
4. Refrigerate for 2-3 hours, turning the chicken halfway through.
5. Cook chicken as desired and discard any leftover marinade.

SMOKY PAPRIKA MARINADE FOR PORK

INGREDIENTS

- 1/3 cup olive oil
- 1/4 cup apple cider vinegar
- 2 tablespoons smoked paprika
- 2 tablespoons honey

- 1 teaspoon garlic powder
- 1 teaspoon onion powder
- Salt and pepper to taste

DIRECTIONS:

1. Combine all ingredients in a bowl, stirring until the honey dissolves.
2. Place pork cuts in a plastic bag or marinating container.
3. Pour the marinade over the pork, ensuring it is evenly distributed.
4. Marinate in the refrigerator for at least 1 hour or up to 8 hours.
5. Cook pork according to preference and discard any remaining marinade.

CITRUS AND DILL MARINADE FOR FISH

INGREDIENTS

- 1/4 cup olive oil
- 1/4 cup fresh orange juice
- 2 tablespoons lemon juice
- 1/4 cup fresh dill, chopped

- 2 cloves garlic, minced
- Zest of one lemon
- Salt and pepper to taste

DIRECTIONS:

1. Whisk together olive oil, orange juice, lemon juice, dill, garlic, lemon zest, salt, and pepper in a bowl.
2. Lay fish fillets in a shallow baking dish.
3. Pour marinade over the fish, ensuring all pieces are covered.
4. Marinate in the refrigerator for 30 minutes.
5. Cook fish as desired, discarding any leftover marinade.

HERB AND GARLIC MARINADE FOR FISH

INGREDIENTS

- 1/3 cup extra virgin olive oil
- 1/4 cup chopped fresh parsley
- 1/4 cup chopped fresh basil

- 3 cloves garlic, minced
- 2 tablespoons lemon juice
- Salt and pepper to taste

DIRECTIONS:

1. Combine olive oil, parsley, basil, garlic, and lemon juice in a bowl. Season with salt and pepper.
2. Place fish fillets or steaks in a glass dish or a resealable plastic bag.
3. Pour the marinade over the fish, ensuring good coverage.
4. Marinate in the refrigerator for 15-30 minutes, not longer to avoid the fish becoming mushy.
5. Cook the fish as preferred and discard the used marinade.

EASY LEMON AND HERB MARINADE FOR SEAFOOD

INGREDIENTS

- 1/4 cup extra virgin olive oil
- Juice of 2 lemons
- 2 cloves garlic, minced
- 2 tablespoons fresh parsley, finely chopped

- 1 teaspoon dried dill (or 1 tablespoon fresh dill, chopped)
- Salt and freshly ground black pepper, to taste

DIRECTIONS:

1. Whisk together olive oil, lemon juice, garlic, parsley, and dill in a bowl; season with salt and pepper.
2. Place seafood in a dish or bag and cover with marinade.
3. Refrigerate for 15-20 minutes.
4. Remove seafood from marinade and cook as desired.

Mediterranean Stuffed Bell Peppers with Eggs and Herbs

Breakfast

AVOCADO AND TOMATO TOAST WITH OLIVE OIL DRIZZLE

 5 Mins ⏳ 2 Mins 👥 Serves: 2

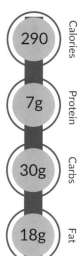
290 Calories
7g Protein
30g Carbs
18g Fat

INGREDIENTS

- 2 slices whole grain bread
- 1 ripe avocado
- 1 medium tomato, sliced
- 1 tablespoon extra virgin olive oil
- Salt and pepper to taste
- Optional garnish: crushed red pepper or fresh herbs (basil, parsley)

DIRECTIONS:

1. Toast the bread until golden and crispy.
2. Mash the peeled and pitted avocado in a bowl until creamy with some chunks.
3. Spread the avocado on the toasted bread and top with tomato slices.
4. Season with salt and pepper, drizzle with olive oil, and add optional garnishes.
5. Serve immediately for optimal flavor and texture.

TOMATO AND FETA TOAST WITH OLIVE OIL DRIZZLE

 5 Mins ⏳ 5 Mins 👥 Serves: 2

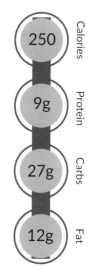
250 Calories
9g Protein
27g Carbs
12g Fat

INGREDIENTS

- 2 slices whole grain bread
- 1 medium tomato, sliced
- 1/4 cup feta cheese, crumbled
- 1 tablespoon extra virgin olive oil
- Fresh basil leaves, for garnish (optional)
- Black pepper, to taste

DIRECTIONS:

1. Toast bread until golden and crispy.
2. Arrange tomato slices on each toast.
3. Sprinkle with crumbled feta.
4. Drizzle with olive oil.
5. Garnish with basil and black pepper, then serve immediately.

RICOTTA AND LEMON PANCAKES

🕐 10 Mins ⏳ 10 Mins 👥 Serves: 2

INGREDIENTS

- 1/2 cup ricotta cheese
- 1/2 cup all-purpose flour
- 1/2 teaspoon baking powder
- 2 tablespoons sugar
- 1 large egg
- 1/4 cup milk
- Zest of 1 lemon
- 1 tablespoon lemon juice
- 1 tablespoon unsalted butter, melted

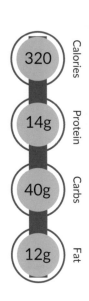
320 Calories
14g Protein
40g Carbs
12g Fat

DIRECTIONS:

1. In a bowl, combine flour, baking powder, and sugar.
2. In another bowl, whisk ricotta, egg, milk, lemon zest, lemon juice, and melted butter until smooth.
3. Add dry ingredients to the wet mix, stirring until just combined.
4. Heat a greased skillet over medium heat. Pour 1/4 cup batter per pancake. Cook until bubbles form, flip, and cook until golden.
5. Enjoy warm with honey or maple syrup if desired.

BANANA AND WALNUT OATMEAL WITH CINNAMON

🕐 5 Mins ⏳ 10 Mins 👥 Serves: 2

INGREDIENTS

- 1 cup low-fat or non-fat Greek yogurt
- 1/2 cup blueberries
- 1/2 cup halved strawberries
- 1/4 cup raspberries
- 1 sliced small banana
- 1 tablespoon honey (optional)
- 1/4 cup cold water or almond milk (for thinning, if needed)
- Ice cubes (optional)

190 Calories
12g Protein
28g Carbs
3g Fat

DIRECTIONS:

1. Measure and prepare all ingredients.
2. In a blender, combine Greek yogurt, all berries, banana, honey (if using), and ice cubes (optional).
3. Blend until smooth, adding water or almond milk to adjust thickness if necessary.
4. Serve immediately in two glasses.

MEDITERRANEAN MORNING SMOOTHIE WITH GREEK YOGURT AND BERRIES

| 🕐 5 Mins | ⧗ 0 Mins | 👥 Serves: 2 |

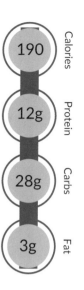

190 Calories
12g Protein
28g Carbs
3g Fat

INGREDIENTS

- 1 cup low-fat or non-fat Greek yogurt
- 1/2 cup blueberries
- 1/2 cup halved strawberries
- 1/4 cup raspberries
- 1 sliced small banana
- 1 tablespoon honey (optional)
- 1/4 cup cold water or almond milk (for thinning, if needed)
- Ice cubes (optional)

DIRECTIONS:

1. Measure and prepare all ingredients.
2. In a blender, combine Greek yogurt, all berries, banana, honey (if using), and ice cubes (optional).
3. Blend until smooth, adding water or almond milk to adjust thickness if necessary.
4. Serve immediately in two glasses.

SPINACH AND FETA BREAKFAST WRAPS

| 🕐 10 Mins | ⧗ 5 Mins | 👥 Serves: 2 |

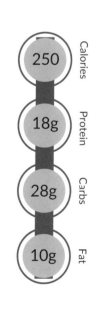

250 Calories
18g Protein
28g Carbs
10g Fat

INGREDIENTS

- 2 whole grain tortillas
- 1 cup fresh spinach, washed and roughly chopped
- 1/2 cup crumbled feta cheese
- 4 egg whites
- 1 small onion, finely chopped
- 1 tablespoon olive oil
- Salt and pepper to taste

DIRECTIONS:

1. In a skillet, heat the olive oil over medium heat. Add onions and sauté until translucent. Add spinach and cook until wilted.
2. In the same skillet, add the egg whites and scramble until fully cooked.
3. Divide the spinach, onion, and scrambled egg whites evenly among the tortillas. Sprinkle feta cheese over each. Roll up the tortillas, cut in half, and serve immediately.

MEDITERRANEAN STUFFED BELL PEPPERS WITH EGGS AND HERBS

🕐 10 Mins ⏳ 20 Mins 👥 Serves: 2

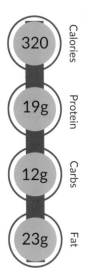

Calories 320
Protein 19g
Carbs 12g
Fat 23g

INGREDIENTS

- 2 large bell peppers, halved and seeded
- 4 eggs
- 1/4 cup crumbled feta cheese
- 1 tablespoon chopped fresh parsley
- 1 tablespoon chopped fresh basil
- 2 tablespoons olive oil
- Salt and pepper to taste

DIRECTIONS:

1. Heat oven to 375°F (190°C). Arrange bell pepper halves on a baking sheet, drizzle with olive oil.
2. Bake for 10 minutes to soften.
3. Crack an egg into each pepper half, season with salt and pepper, and sprinkle with feta, parsley, and basil.
4. Return to oven and bake 10-12 minutes until eggs are set.

ZUCCHINI AND POTATO FRITTATA

🕐 10 Mins ⏳ 20 Mins 👥 Serves: 2

Calories 320
Protein 18g
Carbs 20g
Fat 20g

INGREDIENTS

- 1 small zucchini, thinly sliced
- 1 small potato, thinly sliced
- 4 large eggs
- 1/4 cup milk
- 1/4 cup grated Parmesan cheese
- 2 tablespoons olive oil
- Salt and pepper to taste
- Fresh herbs (like parsley or chives), for garnish

DIRECTIONS:

1. Heat olive oil in a skillet over medium heat. Add potatoes and cook for 5 minutes, then add zucchini and cook until tender.
2. In a bowl, mix eggs, milk, Parmesan, salt, and pepper.
3. Pour eggs over vegetables in the skillet. Cook on low until eggs set and bottom is golden, about 10-12 minutes.
4. Broil for 1-2 minutes to brown the top. Garnish with fresh herbs and serve warm.

TOMATO AND MOZZARELLA STUFFED FRENCH TOAST

15 Mins | 10 Mins | Serves: 2

Calories 350
Protein 18g
Carbs 28g
Fat 18g

INGREDIENTS

- 4 slices of whole grain bread
- 2 large eggs
- 1/4 cup milk
- 1/2 cup shredded mozzarella cheese
- 1 medium tomato, thinly sliced
- 2 teaspoons olive oil
- Salt and pepper to taste
- Fresh basil leaves for garnish

1. Make a pocket in each slice of bread by cutting along one edge.
2. Fill each pocket with mozzarella cheese and tomato slices.
3. In a bowl, whisk together eggs, milk, salt, and pepper.
4. Dip each stuffed bread slice into the egg mixture, ensuring both sides are coated.
5. Heat olive oil in a skillet over medium heat. Add the dipped bread and cook until golden brown on both sides, about 4-5 minutes per side.
6. Garnish with fresh basil and serve warm.

GREEK YOGURT PARFAIT WITH HONEY AND WALNUTS

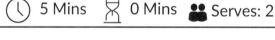

5 Mins | 0 Mins | Serves: 2

Calories 300
Protein 20g
Carbs 24g
Fat 16g

INGREDIENTS

- 2 cups Greek yogurt (low-fat or full-fat based on preference)
- 4 tablespoons honey
- 1/2 cup walnuts, chopped
- Optional: Fresh berries or sliced fruits for layering

DIRECTIONS:

1. Gather all ingredients. If adding fruit, wash and slice as needed.
2. Layer Parfait: In two serving glasses, layer Greek yogurt, a drizzle of honey, and a sprinkle of chopped walnuts. Repeat layers until glasses are filled.
3. Garnish: Top each parfait with a final drizzle of honey and a few walnut pieces.
4. Serve: Enjoy immediately or chill in the refrigerator for an hour before serving for enhanced flavors.

TURKISH MENEMEN (TOMATO AND EGG SCRAMBLE)

 5 Mins ⏳ 10 Mins 👥 Serves: 2

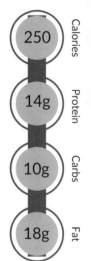

250 Calories
14g Protein
10g Carbs
18g Fat

INGREDIENTS

- 4 large eggs
- 2 large tomatoes, finely chopped
- 1 green bell pepper, chopped
- 1 small onion, chopped
- 2 tablespoons olive oil
- 1/2 teaspoon paprika
- Salt and pepper to taste
- Fresh parsley, chopped (for garnish)

1. In a skillet, heat olive oil over medium heat. Add the chopped onions and green peppers, sautéing until softened, about 3 minutes.
2. Stir in the chopped tomatoes and paprika. Cook until tomatoes are soft and the mixture becomes saucy, about 5 minutes.
3. Crack eggs directly into the skillet. Stir gently, scrambling the eggs with the tomato mixture until the eggs are fully cooked and fluffy.
4. Season with salt and pepper. Garnish with chopped parsley. Serve hot.

ITALIAN BASIL AND TOMATO BRUSCHETTA

⏰ 10 Mins ⏳ 5 Mins 👥 Serves: 2

180 Calories
6g Protein
27g Carbs
7g Fat

INGREDIENTS

- 4 slices of whole-grain baguette
- 2 large ripe tomatoes, chopped
- 1/4 cup fresh basil leaves, chopped
- 2 cloves garlic, minced
- 1 tablespoon extra virgin olive oil
- 1 teaspoon balsamic vinegar
- Salt and pepper to taste

DIRECTIONS:

1. Preheat your oven to 400°F (200°C). Place baguette slices on a baking sheet and toast in the oven until golden, about 5 minutes.
2. Mix Topping: In a bowl, combine the chopped tomatoes, basil, minced garlic, olive oil, and balsamic vinegar. Season with salt and pepper to taste.
3. Assemble Bruschetta: Spoon the tomato mixture generously onto the toasted bread slices.
4. Serve: Enjoy immediately for the best texture and flavor.

CRETAN DAKOS (TOMATO AND CHEESE TOAST)

 10 Mins | 0 Mins | Serves: 2

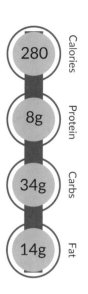

Calories 280
Protein 8g
Carbs 34g
Fat 14g

INGREDIENTS

- 2 barley rusks (or whole-grain bread slices if rusks are unavailable)
- 2 large ripe tomatoes, grated or finely chopped
- 1/2 cup crumbled feta cheese
- 2 tablespoons extra virgin olive oil
- 1 small red onion, finely chopped (optional)
- Fresh basil or oregano leaves, for garnish

DIRECTIONS:

1. Briefly soak the barley rusks in water to soften them slightly, then drain.
2. Mix the grated tomatoes with a pinch of salt and let sit for a few minutes to draw out the juices.
3. Place the softened rusks on plates. Spoon the tomato mixture over each rusk, then sprinkle with chopped onion if using.
4. Top with crumbled feta cheese and a drizzle of olive oil.
5. Finish with fresh basil or oregano. Serve immediately.

AVOCADO EGG SCRAMBLE WRAP

 5 Mins | 5 Mins | Serves: 2

Calories 420
Protein 18g
Carbs 30g
Fat 27g

INGREDIENTS

- 4 eggs
- 1 ripe avocado, mashed
- 2 whole grain tortillas
- 1/2 small onion, diced
- 1 small tomato, diced
- 1 tablespoon olive oil
- Salt and pepper to taste

DIRECTIONS:

1. Beat eggs in a bowl. Stir in the mashed avocado.
2. Heat olive oil in a skillet over medium heat. Add the onion and cook until translucent.
3. Pour the egg and avocado mixture into the skillet. Stir gently until the eggs are softly scrambled.
4. Heat tortillas in a separate pan or in the microwave for 10-15 seconds.
5. Spoon the egg mixture down the center of each tortilla. Top with diced tomato and optional feta or herbs. Fold the tortillas over the filling and serve immediately.

ALMOND BUTTER TOAST DELIGHT

🕐 5 Mins ⏳ 2 Mins 👥 Serves: 2

INGREDIENTS

- 4 slices whole grain bread
- 4 tablespoons almond butter
- 1 banana, sliced
- 2 teaspoons honey
- Optional: sprinkle of chia seeds or sliced almonds

330 Calories

12g Protein

45g Carbs

15g Fat

DIRECTIONS:

1. Toast the whole grain bread slices to your desired crispness.
2. Spread each slice evenly with almond butter.
3. Top each slice with banana slices. Drizzle honey over the top.
4. Sprinkle with chia seeds or sliced almonds for extra crunch and nutrition.
5. Enjoy immediately while warm.

QUICK BERRY OAT CRUNCH

🕐 5 Mins ⏳ 0 Mins 👥 Serves: 2

INGREDIENTS

- 1 cup rolled oats
- 1 cup mixed berries (fresh or frozen)
- 1 cup Greek yogurt (plain or vanilla)
- 2 tablespoons honey
- 2 tablespoons almond slices
- Optional: sprinkle of cinnamon or flax seeds

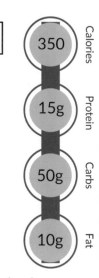

350 Calories

15g Protein

50g Carbs

10g Fat

DIRECTIONS:

1. In two bowls, layer half the oats, followed by half the Greek yogurt, and then a layer of mixed berries.
2. Drizzle each bowl with honey and sprinkle with almond slices. Add a pinch of cinnamon or flax seeds if using.
3. Enjoy immediately for a crunchy texture, or refrigerate overnight for a softer oatmeal-like consistency.

HERBED GOAT CHEESE AND ASPARAGUS FRITTATA

⏱ 10 Mins ⏳ 15 Mins 👥 Serves: 2

320 Calories
22g Protein
4g Carbs
23g Fat

INGREDIENTS

- 6 eggs
- 1/2 cup asparagus, trimmed and cut into 1-inch pieces
- 1/4 cup goat cheese, crumbled
- 2 tablespoons fresh herbs (such as chives and parsley), chopped
- 1 tablespoon olive oil
- Salt and pepper to taste

1. Preheat your oven to 375°F (190°C). Beat eggs in a bowl with salt and pepper.
2. Heat olive oil in an oven-safe skillet over medium heat. Add asparagus and sauté until tender, about 3-4 minutes.
3. Pour the beaten eggs over the asparagus. Cook for 2 minutes until the edges begin to set.
4. Sprinkle goat cheese and chopped herbs over the top.
5. Transfer the skillet to the oven and bake for 10 minutes, or until the eggs are set and lightly golden on top.

PROVENÇAL VEGETABLE OMELETTE

⏱ 10 Mins ⏳ 8 Mins 👥 Serves: 2

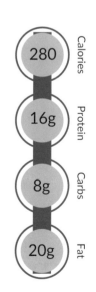

280 Calories
16g Protein
8g Carbs
20g Fat

INGREDIENTS

- 4 large eggs
- 1/2 cup zucchini, thinly sliced
- 1/2 cup bell peppers, assorted colors, thinly sliced
- 1/4 cup red onion, thinly sliced
- 1/4 cup cherry tomatoes, halved
- 1 garlic clove, minced
- 2 tablespoons olive oil
- 1 tablespoon fresh herbs (thyme or basil), chopped
- Optional: 1/4 cup crumbled feta cheese

DIRECTIONS:

1. In a skillet with olive oil over medium heat, cook zucchini, bell peppers, onion, and garlic until tender (3-4 minutes).
2. Whisk eggs with salt, pepper, and herbs in a bowl.
3. Add more oil to the skillet. Pour in the egg mixture; cook until the edges set (about 3 minutes).
4. Top with tomatoes and feta. Cover and cook until eggs are set (2-3 minutes).

OLIVE AND TOMATO MORNING FLATBREAD

 10 Mins ⏳ 10 Mins 👥 Serves: 2

INGREDIENTS

- 2 pre-made flatbreads
- 1/2 cup cherry tomatoes, halved
- 1/4 cup black olives, sliced
- 1/4 cup feta cheese, crumbled
- 2 tablespoons olive oil
- 1 teaspoon dried oregano
- Salt and pepper to taste
- Fresh basil leaves, for garnish

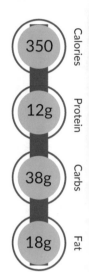

350 Calories
12g Protein
38g Carbs
18g Fat

1. Heat your oven to 400°F (200°C).
2. Prepare Flatbreads: Place flatbreads on a baking sheet.
3. Add Toppings: Drizzle each flatbread with olive oil. Evenly distribute tomatoes, olives, and feta cheese on top. Sprinkle with oregano, salt, and pepper.
4. Bake: Cook in the oven for about 10 minutes until the edges are crispy and the cheese is slightly melted.
5. Garnish and Serve: Remove from the oven, add fresh basil, and serve immediately.

SIMPLE GREEK BERRY BOWL

⏱ 5 Mins ⏳ 0 Mins 👥 Serves: 2

INGREDIENTS

- 1 cup Greek yogurt (plain or vanilla)
- 1 cup mixed berries (blueberries, strawberries, raspberries)
- 2 tablespoons honey
- 1/4 cup granola
- 2 tablespoons chopped nuts (almonds or walnuts)
- Optional: mint leaves for garnish

250 Calories
10g Protein
35g Carbs
8g Fat

DIRECTIONS:

1. Wash and prepare the berries. If using strawberries, slice them.
2. Assemble Bowl: In two bowls, divide the Greek yogurt.
3. Add Berries: Top each bowl of yogurt with an even amount of mixed berries.
4. Drizzle Honey: Drizzle each bowl with honey.
5. Add Crunch: Sprinkle granola and chopped nuts over the top.
6. Garnish and Serve: Add mint leaves if using, and serve immediately.

Small Plates

The "Small Plates" chapter features a collection of appetizer-sized dishes perfect for sharing or sampling different flavors. It includes diverse recipes from tapas to mezze and antipasti, focusing on fresh ingredients and bold seasonings, ideal for entertaining or casual meals.

TOMATO AND MOZZARELLA CAPRESE SKEWERS

🕐 10 Mins	⏳ 0 Mins	👥 Serves: 2

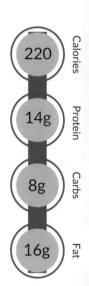

220 Calories
14g Protein
8g Carbs
16g Fat

INGREDIENTS

- 1 large tomato, cut into 8 small chunks
- 8 small balls of fresh mozzarella cheese
- 8 fresh basil leaves
- 2 tablespoons balsamic reduction
- 2 teaspoons olive oil
- Salt and pepper to taste

DIRECTIONS:

1. Thread a tomato chunk, a basil leaf, and a mozzarella ball onto each skewer. Repeat until all ingredients are used.
2. Drizzle with olive oil and balsamic reduction, then sprinkle with salt and pepper.
3. Arrange skewers on a plate and serve immediately.

MUSHROOM AND GARLIC CROSTINI

🕐 10 Mins	⏳ 10 Mins	👥 Serves: 2

250 Calories
10g Protein
35g Carbs
8g Fat

INGREDIENTS

- 4 slices of whole grain baguette
- 1 cup sliced mushrooms (such as cremini or button)
- 2 cloves garlic, minced
- 2 tablespoons olive oil
- 2 tablespoons grated Parmesan cheese
- Fresh thyme or parsley for garnish
- Salt and pepper to taste

DIRECTIONS:

1. Set oven to 375°F (190°C).
2. Brush baguette slices with 1 tablespoon olive oil and toast until golden, about 5-7 minutes.
3. In a skillet, heat the remaining olive oil, add garlic and mushrooms, and sauté until golden, about 5 minutes. Season with salt and pepper.
4. Place mushroom mixture on toasted bread, top with Parmesan.
5. Broil for 2-3 minutes until cheese melts. Add fresh thyme or parsley and serve.

MARINATED OLIVES WITH CITRUS AND HERBS

🕐 5 Mins	⏳ 0 Mins	👥 Serves: 2

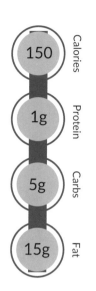

150 Calories
1g Protein
5g Carbs
15g Fat

INGREDIENTS

- 1 cup mixed olives (green and black)
- 1 tablespoon olive oil
- Zest of 1 lemon
- Zest of 1 orange
- 1 garlic clove, minced
- 1 tablespoon fresh rosemary, chopped
- 1 tablespoon fresh thyme, chopped
- 1/2 teaspoon red pepper flakes (optional)
- Salt and pepper to taste

1. In a bowl, mix together the olives, olive oil, lemon zest, orange zest, garlic, rosemary, thyme, and red pepper flakes.
2. Add salt and pepper to taste, tossing to coat evenly.
3. Cover and let the olives marinate in the fridge for at least 30 minutes to allow the flavors to meld.
4. Bring to room temperature before serving.

SPANAKOPITA BITES (MINI SPINACH PIES)

🕐 10 Mins	⏳ 15 Mins	👥 Serves: 2

200 Calories
8g Protein
22g Carbs
10g Fat

- 1 cup fresh spinach, chopped
- 1/4 cup crumbled feta cheese
- 1 tablespoon Greek yogurt
- 1 tablespoon olive oil
- 1 small garlic clove, minced
- 4 sheets phyllo dough, thawed
- Salt and pepper to taste
- 1 tablespoon melted butter or olive oil (for brushing)

1. In a pan, heat olive oil over medium heat. Add garlic and spinach, cooking until wilted. Remove from heat and mix in feta, Greek yogurt, salt, and pepper.
2. Cut the phyllo dough sheets into squares, about 4x4 inches.
3. Place a spoonful of the spinach mixture onto each phyllo square. Fold the dough over to form triangles, sealing the edges by brushing with melted butter or olive oil.
4. Place the bites on a baking sheet and bake at 350°F (175°C) for 10-15 minutes, or until golden and crispy.
5. Remove from the oven and serve warm.

ARTICHOKE AND SPINACH DIP WITH GRILLED FLATBREAD

🕐 8 Mins ⏳ 12 Mins 👥 Serves: 2

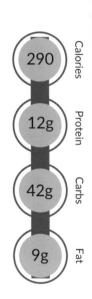

290 Calories

12g Protein

42g Carbs

9g Fat

- 1 cup fresh spinach, chopped
- 1/2 cup canned artichoke hearts, drained and chopped
- 1/4 cup Greek yogurt
- 1/4 cup feta cheese, crumbled
- 1/4 cup grated Parmesan cheese
- 1 garlic clove, minced
- 1 teaspoon olive oil
- 1/4 teaspoon black pepper
- 1/4 teaspoon dried oregano
- 2 store-bought whole wheat flatbreads

1. Preheat oven to 375°F (190°C).
2. In a bowl, mix Greek yogurt, feta, Parmesan, spinach, artichokes, garlic, olive oil, black pepper, and oregano.
3. Transfer the mixture to a baking dish and bake for 12-15 minutes, until bubbly and golden on top.
4. Warm the store-bought flatbread in the oven or grill for 1-2 minutes.
5. Serve the dip warm with the flatbread on the side for dipping.

SAGANAKI (FLAMING GREEK CHEESE) WITH LEMON

🕐 5 Mins ⏳ 5 Mins 👥 Serves: 2

280 Calories

16g Protein

2g Carbs

22g Fat

INGREDIENTS
- 4 ounces kefalotyri or graviera cheese, cut into 1/2-inch-thick slices
- 1 tablespoon all-purpose flour
- 1 tablespoon olive oil
- 1 tablespoon brandy (optional for flaming)
- 1 lemon, cut into wedges
- Fresh parsley, chopped (for garnish)

DIRECTIONS:
1. Lightly dust the cheese slices with flour, shaking off any excess.
2. Heat olive oil in a skillet over medium heat. Add the cheese and cook for about 2 minutes on each side, until golden brown and crispy.
3. For the flaming effect, carefully pour the brandy over the cheese while it's in the skillet. Ignite with a lighter or match (make sure to do this safely). Once the flames subside, immediately squeeze lemon juice over the cheese.
4. Transfer to a serving plate, garnish with fresh parsley, and serve with lemon wedges.

GRILLED SARDINES WITH LEMON AND GARLIC

| 🕐 10 Mins | ⧖ 8 Mins | 👥 Serves: 2 |

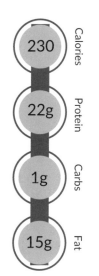

230 Calories
22g Protein
1g Carbs
15g Fat

INGREDIENTS

- 6 fresh sardines, cleaned and gutted
- 2 tablespoons olive oil
- 2 garlic cloves, minced
- 1 tablespoon lemon juice
- 1 teaspoon lemon zest
- Salt and pepper to taste
- Fresh parsley, chopped (for garnish)
- Lemon wedges (for serving)

1. In a small bowl, mix olive oil, garlic, lemon juice, lemon zest, salt, and pepper. Rub this mixture over the sardines, ensuring they're well coated. Let marinate for 10 minutes.
2. Heat the grill to medium-high heat.
3. Place the sardines on the grill and cook for 3-4 minutes per side, or until the skin is crispy and the flesh is cooked through.
4. Remove from the grill, garnish with fresh parsley, and serve with lemon wedges.

SPICY FETA DIP (TIROKAFTERI)

| 🕐 10 Mins | ⧖ 0 Mins | 👥 Serves: 2 |

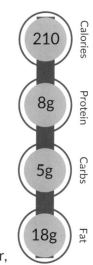

210 Calories
8g Protein
5g Carbs
18g Fat

- 1 cup feta cheese, crumbled
- 2 tablespoons Greek yogurt
- 1 tablespoon olive oil
- 1 teaspoon lemon juice
- 1 small red chili pepper, chopped (or 1/2 teaspoon red pepper flakes)
- 1 garlic clove, minced
- 1/2 teaspoon paprika
- Fresh parsley, for garnish

1. In a food processor, combine feta cheese, Greek yogurt, olive oil, lemon juice, chili pepper, garlic, and paprika. Blend until smooth.
2. Adjust Seasoning: Taste and adjust for heat or acidity by adding more chili or lemon juice if desired.
3. Chill: Transfer the dip to a serving bowl and chill for 10 minutes.
4. Garnish and Serve: Garnish with fresh parsley and a drizzle of olive oil. Serve with pita bread or vegetables.

SMOKED SALMON AND CREAM CHEESE ROLL-UPS

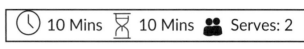

| 🕐 10 Mins | ⧖ 10 Mins | 👥 Serves: 2 |

INGREDIENTS

- 4 slices smoked salmon
- 4 tablespoons cream cheese
- 1 tablespoon capers, drained
- 1 teaspoon fresh dill, chopped
- 1 teaspoon lemon zest
- 1 teaspoon olive oil (optional)

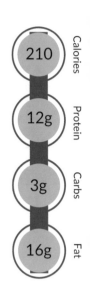

210 Calories
12g Protein
3g Carbs
16g Fat

DIRECTIONS:

1. In a small bowl, mix the cream cheese, capers, dill, and lemon zest until well combined.
2. Lay the smoked salmon slices flat. Spread the cream cheese mixture evenly over each slice.
3. Gently roll up each slice, starting from one end, to form a roll-up.
4. Arrange on a plate and drizzle with a little olive oil if desired. Serve immediately.

ROASTED GARLIC AND WHITE BEAN DIP

| 🕐 10 Mins | ⧖ 20 Mins | 👥 Serves: 2 |

- 1/2 cup dry green or brown lentils
- 2 cups fresh spinach, chopped
- 1 small red onion, thinly sliced
- 1/4 cup crumbled feta cheese
- 1 tablespoon olive oil
- 1 tablespoon fresh lemon juice
- 1 tablespoon fresh orange juice
- 1 teaspoon Dijon mustard
- Salt and pepper to taste

230 Calories
10g Protein
28g Carbs
8g Fat

1. In a small pot, bring lentils and 1 cup water to a boil. Reduce heat and simmer for 15-20 minutes, or until lentils are tender. Drain and let cool.
2. In a small bowl, whisk together olive oil, lemon juice, orange juice, Dijon mustard, salt, and pepper.
3. In a large bowl, combine cooled lentils, chopped spinach, and sliced red onion.
4. Pour the citrus dressing over the salad and toss to coat.
5. Top with crumbled feta cheese and optional chopped parsley. Serve immediately.

BAKED RICOTTA WITH LEMON AND THYME

| ⏱ 5 Mins | ⏳ 15 Mins | 👥 Serves: 2 |

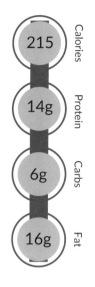

215 Calories
14g Protein
6g Carbs
16g Fat

INGREDIENTS

- 1 cup ricotta cheese
- Zest of 1 lemon
- 1 tablespoon fresh thyme leaves, chopped
- 1 tablespoon olive oil
- Salt and pepper to taste

DIRECTIONS:

1. Preheat Oven: Heat oven to 375°F (190°C).
2. Prepare Ricotta: In a bowl, combine ricotta with lemon zest, thyme, and a pinch of salt and pepper.
3. Bake: Transfer the mixture to a small baking dish, drizzle with olive oil, and bake until golden and set, about 15 minutes.
4. Serve: Enjoy warm, perhaps with a side of whole-grain toast or fresh vegetables.

GARLIC SHRIMP SKEWERS

| ⏱ 6 Mins | ⏳ 10 Mins | 👥 Serves: 2 |

180 Calories
24g Protein
4g Carbs
8g Fat

INGREDIENTS

- 12 large shrimp, peeled and deveined
- 2 cloves garlic, minced
- 1 tablespoon olive oil
- 1 lemon, juiced and zested
- 1/2 teaspoon paprika
- Salt and pepper to taste
- Fresh parsley, chopped (for garnish)

DIRECTIONS:

1. In a bowl, mix garlic, olive oil, lemon juice, lemon zest, paprika, salt, and pepper. Add shrimp and toss to coat. Let marinate for 10 minutes.
2. Heat a grill or grill pan over medium-high heat.
3. Thread shrimp onto skewers.
4. Grill skewers for about 3 minutes per side or until shrimp are opaque and slightly charred.
5. Garnish with fresh parsley and serve with lemon wedges on the side.

ZUCCHINI FRITTERS WITH YOGURT DIP

🕐 15 Mins ⏳ 10 Mins 👥 Serves: 2

- 2 medium zucchinis, grated
- 1/4 cup all-purpose flour (or almond flour for a lower carb option)
- 1 large egg
- 2 tablespoons chopped green onions
- 1 clove garlic, minced
- Salt and pepper to taste
- 2 tablespoons olive oil for frying
- 1/2 cup plain Greek yogurt
- 1 tablespoon fresh dill, chopped
- 1 teaspoon lemon zest

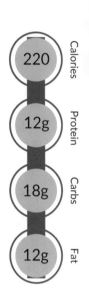

220	Calories
12g	Protein
18g	Carbs
12g	Fat

1. Squeeze excess moisture out of the grated zucchini using a clean cloth or paper towels.
2. In a bowl, combine the dried zucchini, flour, egg, green onions, garlic, salt, and pepper.
3. Warm olive oil in a skillet over medium heat.
4. Scoop tablespoons of the zucchini mixture into the skillet, flatten slightly, and fry until golden brown, about 2-3 minutes per side.
5. Mix Greek yogurt, dill, and lemon zest in a small bowl.
6. Serve fritters hot with yogurt dip on the side.

MARINATED FETA WITH OLIVES

🕐 10 Mins ⏳ 0 Mins 👥 Serves: 2

INGREDIENTS
- 1 cup feta cheese, cubed
- 1/2 cup mixed olives
- 1/4 cup olive oil
- 2 cloves garlic, thinly sliced
- 1 teaspoon dried oregano
- 1 teaspoon dried thyme
- Zest of 1 lemon
- Freshly ground black pepper to taste

320	Calories
10g	Protein
5g	Carbs
30g	Fat

DIRECTIONS:
1. In a mixing bowl, combine feta cheese, olives, olive oil, garlic slices, dried oregano, thyme, and lemon zest.
2. Marinate: Toss gently to coat all the ingredients evenly. Let the mixture marinate at room temperature for about 20 minutes to blend the flavors.
3. Serve: Transfer to a serving dish, sprinkle with freshly ground black pepper, and serve with crusty bread or as part of a breakfast spread.

MINTY CUCUMBER CUPS

🕐 10 Mins	⧖ 0 Mins	👥 Serves: 2

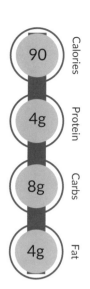

Calories 90
Protein 4g
Carbs 8g
Fat 4g

INGREDIENTS

- 1 large cucumber
- 1/2 cup Greek yogurt
- 2 tablespoons fresh mint, finely chopped
- 1 small garlic clove, minced
- 1 tablespoon lemon juice
- Salt and pepper to taste
- Optional: diced tomatoes or olives for garnish

DIRECTIONS:

1. Slice the cucumber into thick rounds (about 1 inch thick). Using a melon baller or small spoon, scoop out the centers to create cups.
2. In a small bowl, combine Greek yogurt, chopped mint, minced garlic, and lemon juice. Season with salt and pepper to taste.
3. Spoon the yogurt mixture into the hollowed-out cucumber cups.
4. Garnish with diced tomatoes or olives if desired. Serve chilled.

OLIVE TAPENADE CROSTINI

🕐 10 Mins	⧖ 5 Mins	👥 Serves: 2

Calories 220
Protein 3g
Carbs 20g
Fat 14g

INGREDIENTS

- 1 cup mixed olives, pitted and chopped
- 1 clove garlic, minced
- 2 tablespoons capers, rinsed and chopped
- 2 tablespoons olive oil
- 1 teaspoon lemon zest
- 1 tablespoon lemon juice
- 1/4 teaspoon freshly ground black pepper
- 4 slices of baguette, toasted

DIRECTIONS:

1. In a food processor, combine olives, garlic, capers, olive oil, lemon zest, and lemon juice. Pulse until mixture becomes a coarse paste.
2. Toast slices of baguette until golden and crispy.
3. Spread a generous amount of olive tapenade over each toasted bread slice.
4. Garnish with a sprinkle of black pepper and a drizzle of olive oil if desired. Serve immediately.

MEDITERRANEAN SHRIMP COCKTAIL

 10 Mins  5 Mins 👥 Serves: 2

- 1/2 pound cooked shrimp, peeled and deveined
- 1/2 cup cucumber, diced
- 1/2 cup cherry tomatoes, halved
- 1/4 cup red onion, finely chopped
- 1/4 cup kalamata olives, pitted and sliced
- 1 tablespoon fresh parsley, chopped
- 2 tablespoons extra virgin olive oil
- 1 tablespoon lemon juice
- Salt and pepper to taste
- Lemon wedges for serving

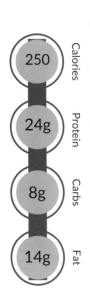

250 Calories
24g Protein
8g Carbs
14g Fat

DIRECTIONS:

1. In a bowl, combine the shrimp, cucumber, cherry tomatoes, red onion, and kalamata olives.
2. Add olive oil, lemon juice, and chopped parsley to the bowl. Season with salt and pepper. Toss gently to coat everything evenly.
3. Refrigerate the mixture for at least 30 minutes to allow flavors to meld.
4. Divide the shrimp cocktail into serving dishes. Serve chilled with lemon wedges on the side.

CRISPY FALAFEL BALLS

🕐 15 Mins ⏳ 10 Mins 👥 Serves: 2

INGREDIENTS
- 1 cup dried chickpeas, soaked overnight
- 1 small onion, chopped
- 2 cloves garlic, minced
- 1/4 cup fresh parsley, chopped
- 1 teaspoon ground cumin
- 1 teaspoon ground coriander
- 1/2 teaspoon salt
- 1/4 teaspoon black pepper
- 1/4 teaspoon baking soda
- Oil for frying
- Optional: tahini sauce for serving

330 Calories
13g Protein
35g Carbs
15g Fat

DIRECTIONS:
1. Drain soaked chickpeas and pat dry.
2. In a food processor, combine chickpeas, onion, garlic, parsley, cumin, coriander, salt, and pepper. Pulse until mixture is finely ground.
3. Stir baking soda into the chickpea mixture. Form into small balls or patties about the size of a walnut.
4. Heat oil in a deep skillet or fryer. Fry falafel balls in batches until golden and crispy, about 4-5 minutes. Drain on paper towels and serve hot with tahini sauce if desired.

GREEK MEATBALLS WITH TZATZIKI

🕐 10 Mins ⏳ 15 Mins 👥 Serves: 2

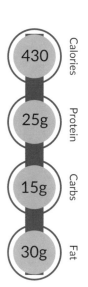

430 — Calories
25g — Protein
15g — Carbs
30g — Fat

INGREDIENTS

- 1/2 pound ground lamb or beef
- 1/4 cup finely chopped onion
- 1 clove garlic, minced
- 2 tablespoons breadcrumbs
- 1 egg
- 1 tablespoon chopped fresh mint
- 1 tablespoon chopped fresh parsley
- 1 teaspoon dried oregano
- Salt and pepper, to taste
- Olive oil for cooking
- 1/2 cup tzatziki sauce for serving

DIRECTIONS:

1. In a bowl, mix ground meat, onion, garlic, breadcrumbs, egg, mint, parsley, oregano, salt, and pepper.
2. Form Meatballs: Shape into small balls, about 1 inch in diameter.
3. Cook Meatballs: Heat a little olive oil in a skillet over medium heat. Add meatballs and cook for about 12-15 minutes, turning occasionally until evenly browned and cooked through.
4. Plate meatballs and serve with a side of tzatziki sauce.

ROASTED RED PEPPER DIP

🕐 5 Mins ⏳ 20 Mins 👥 Serves: 2

190 — Calories
4g — Protein
12g — Carbs
14g — Fat

INGREDIENTS

- 2 large red bell peppers
- 1 clove garlic
- 2 tablespoons olive oil
- 1/4 cup feta cheese, crumbled
- 1 tablespoon lemon juice
- 1/2 teaspoon smoked paprika
- Salt and pepper to taste

1. Preheat your oven to 425°F (220°C). Place whole bell peppers on a baking sheet and roast until the skins are charred and blistered, about 20 minutes. Remove from oven and cover with aluminum foil for 5 minutes to steam.
2. Peel the skins from the peppers, remove the seeds, and chop the flesh.
3. In a blender or food processor, combine roasted peppers, garlic, olive oil, feta cheese, lemon juice, and smoked paprika. Blend until smooth.
4. Taste and adjust seasoning with salt and pepper.
5. Transfer to a serving bowl and serve with toasted pita bread or fresh vegetables.

Soup & Salad

SMOKED SALMON AND AVOCADO CAESAR SALAD

 10 Mins 0 Mins Serves: 2

INGREDIENTS

- 4 ounces smoked salmon, sliced
- 1 ripe avocado, sliced
- 4 cups romaine lettuce, chopped
- 1/4 cup Caesar dressing (low-sodium preferred)
- 2 tablespoons grated Parmesan cheese
- 1 tablespoon capers
- Lemon wedges for serving

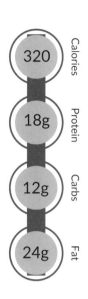

Calories 320
Protein 18g
Carbs 12g
Fat 24g

DIRECTIONS:

1. Wash and chop the romaine lettuce. Slice the avocado and smoked salmon.
2. In a large bowl, toss the romaine lettuce with Caesar dressing until evenly coated.
3. Arrange smoked salmon and avocado slices on top of the dressed lettuce.
4. Sprinkle with Parmesan cheese and capers.
5. Serve the salad with lemon wedges on the side.

TOMATO BASIL SOUP WITH A TOUCH OF CREAM

🕐 5 Mins ⧖ 20 Mins 👥 Serves: 2

INGREDIENTS

- 4 large tomatoes, peeled and diced
- 1 onion, chopped
- 2 cloves garlic, minced
- 1 cup low-sodium vegetable broth
- 1/4 cup fresh basil leaves, chopped
- 2 tablespoons heavy cream
- 1 tablespoon olive oil
- Salt and pepper to taste

Calories 180
Protein 3g
Carbs 20g
Fat 10g

1. In a pot, heat olive oil over medium heat. Add onions and garlic, sauté until softened, about 5 minutes.
2. Add tomatoes and vegetable broth, bring to a boil, then reduce heat and simmer for 15 minutes.
3. Puree the soup in a blender or use an immersion blender until smooth.
4. Return soup to the pot, stir in cream and basil, and heat through. Season with salt and pepper. Serve hot

ROASTED RED PEPPER AND FETA SALAD WITH FRESH HERBS

| ⏰ 10 Mins | ⏳ 15 Mins | 👥 Serves: 2 |

INGREDIENTS

- 2 large red bell peppers
- 1/4 cup crumbled feta cheese
- 1 tablespoon olive oil
- 1 tablespoon balsamic vinegar
- 1 tablespoon fresh parsley, chopped
- 1 tablespoon fresh basil, chopped
- Salt and pepper to taste
- Optional: 1 teaspoon capers

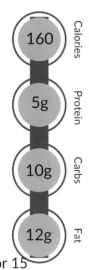

160 Calories
5g Protein
10g Carbs
12g Fat

1. Preheat the oven to 400°F (200°C). Place whole red peppers on a baking sheet and roast for 15 minutes, turning once, until skins are charred.
2. Remove from the oven and let cool. Peel off the skins and slice peppers into thin strips.
3. In a small bowl, whisk together olive oil, balsamic vinegar, salt, and pepper.
4. Arrange roasted red pepper strips on a serving plate. Sprinkle with crumbled feta cheese, fresh parsley, basil, and optional capers.
5. Drizzle the dressing over the salad and serve immediately.

LENTIL AND SPINACH SALAD WITH CITRUS DRESSING

| ⏰ 10 Mins | ⏳ 20 Mins | 👥 Serves: 2 |

- 1/2 cup dry green or brown lentils
- 2 cups fresh spinach, chopped
- 1 small red onion, thinly sliced
- 1/4 cup crumbled feta cheese
- 1 tablespoon olive oil
- 1 tablespoon fresh lemon juice
- 1 tablespoon fresh orange juice
- 1 teaspoon Dijon mustard
- Salt and pepper to taste

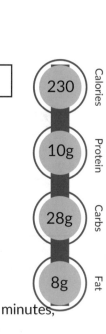

230 Calories
10g Protein
28g Carbs
8g Fat

1. In a small pot, bring lentils and 1 cup water to a boil. Reduce heat and simmer for 15-20 minutes, or until lentils are tender. Drain and let cool.
2. In a small bowl, whisk together olive oil, lemon juice, orange juice, Dijon mustard, salt, and pepper.
3. In a large bowl, combine cooled lentils, chopped spinach, and sliced red onion.
4. Pour the citrus dressing over the salad and toss to coat.
5. Top with crumbled feta cheese and optional chopped parsley. Serve immediately.

MEDITERRANEAN QUINOA SALAD WITH BELL PEPPERS AND OLIVES

| ⏱ 10 Mins | ⧗ 0 Mins | 👥 Serves: 2 |

- 1/2 cup quinoa, uncooked
- 1 cup water
- 1 red bell pepper, diced
- 1/4 cup sliced black olives
- 1/4 cup crumbled feta cheese
- 2 tablespoons olive oil
- 1 tablespoon red wine vinegar
- 1/2 teaspoon dried oregano
- Salt and pepper to taste
- Fresh parsley, chopped (for garnish)

320 Calories
18g Protein
12g Carbs
24g Fat

1. Rinse quinoa, boil in water, reduce heat, cover, and simmer for 15 minutes until water is absorbed.
2. Dice bell pepper and slice olives while quinoa cooks.
3. Whisk olive oil, vinegar, oregano, salt, and pepper.
4. Fluff quinoa, mix in bell peppers, olives, and feta, then toss with dressing.
5. Garnish with parsley and serve warm or chilled.

HEARTY CHICKPEA AND SPINACH SOUP

| ⏱ 10 Mins | ⧗ 20 Mins | 👥 Serves: 2 |

INGREDIENTS

- 1 can (15 oz) chickpeas, drained and rinsed
- 2 cups fresh spinach, roughly chopped
- 1 small onion, diced
- 2 cloves garlic, minced
- 4 cups low-sodium vegetable broth
- 1 teaspoon olive oil
- 1/2 teaspoon ground cumin
- Salt and pepper to taste
- Lemon wedges for serving

295 Calories
14g Protein
45g Carbs
7g Fat

DIRECTIONS:

1. Heat olive oil in a pot over medium heat. Add onion and garlic, sautéing until onion is translucent.
2. Stir in chickpeas and cumin, cooking for 1-2 minutes to enhance flavors.
3. Pour in vegetable broth, bring to a boil, then reduce heat and simmer for 15 minutes.
4. Stir in spinach and cook until wilted, about 3 minutes.
5. Adjust seasoning with salt and pepper. Serve hot with lemon wedges on the side.

GRILLED EGGPLANT AND MOZZARELLA SALAD

🕐 15 Mins ⏳ 10 Mins 👥 Serves: 2

250	Calories
12g	Protein
15g	Carbs
18g	Fat

INGREDIENTS

- 1 large eggplant, sliced into 1/2-inch rounds
- 4 ounces fresh mozzarella cheese, sliced
- 2 tablespoons olive oil
- 1 tablespoon balsamic vinegar
- 1/2 cup fresh basil leaves
- Salt and pepper to taste
- Cooking spray for grilling

1. Brush eggplant with olive oil, season with salt and pepper.
2. Heat grill or pan, spray with cooking spray, and grill eggplant 3-4 minutes per side until tender.
3. Layer grilled eggplant on a plate, top with mozzarella and basil.
4. Drizzle with balsamic vinegar and extra olive oil.
5. Serve the salad warm or at room temperature.

ZUCCHINI RIBBON SALAD WITH LEMON AND PARMESAN

🕐 10 Mins ⏳ 20 Mins 👥 Serves: 2

180	Calories
3g	Protein
20g	Carbs
10g	Fat

INGREDIENTS

- 2 medium zucchinis
- 1 lemon, zested and juiced
- 1/4 cup shaved Parmesan cheese
- 2 tablespoons olive oil
- Salt and pepper to taste
- Fresh basil leaves, for garnish

DIRECTIONS:

1. Using a vegetable peeler, slice zucchinis into long, thin ribbons.
2. In a bowl, combine lemon zest, lemon juice, olive oil, salt, and pepper. Toss zucchini ribbons in the dressing to coat.
3. Arrange dressed zucchini on plates, top with shaved Parmesan and basil leaves.
4. Serve immediately, or chill briefly for enhanced flavors.

WILD MUSHROOM AND LEEK CHOWDER WITH THYME

INGREDIENTS

⏱ 5 Mins ⧗ 15 Mins 👥 Serves: 2

270 Calories
6g Protein
15g Carbs
22g Fat

- 1 cup wild mushrooms, chopped (such as shiitake, oyster, and cremini)
- 1 leek, white and light green parts only, finely chopped
- 2 cloves garlic, minced
- 2 cups low-sodium vegetable broth
- 1/2 cup heavy cream
- 1 tablespoon fresh thyme leaves
- 1 tablespoon olive oil
- Salt and pepper to taste

DIRECTIONS:

1. In a pot, heat olive oil over medium heat. Add leeks and garlic, sauté until soft, about 5 minutes.
2. Stir in mushrooms and cook until they begin to brown, about 8 minutes.
3. Add vegetable broth and thyme. Bring to a simmer and cook for 10 minutes.
4. Stir in heavy cream, season with salt and pepper, and heat through without boiling.
5. Serve hot, garnished with additional thyme if desired.

EASY GAZPACHO

⏱ 15 Mins ⧗ 0 Mins 👥 Serves: 2

INGREDIENTS

180 Calories
4g Protein
28g Carbs
7g Fat

- 3 ripe tomatoes, roughly chopped
- 1 cucumber, peeled and chopped
- 1 bell pepper, seeded and chopped
- 1 small red onion, chopped
- 2 cloves garlic, minced
- 2 cups tomato juice (low sodium)
- 2 tablespoons red wine vinegar
- 1 tablespoon olive oil
- Salt and pepper to taste
- Fresh herbs like parsley or cilantro for garnish

DIRECTIONS:

1. In a blender, combine tomatoes, cucumber, bell pepper, onion, and garlic.
2. Pulse until the mixture is smooth, depending on your texture preference.
3. Add tomato juice, vinegar, and olive oil. Season with salt and pepper, then blend again.
4. Refrigerate the gazpacho for at least 1 hour to allow flavors to meld.
5. Serve chilled, garnished with fresh herbs.

SIMPLE GREEK SALAD WITH CUCUMBER, TOMATO, AND FETA

⏱ 10 Mins	⧖ 0 Mins	👥 Serves: 2

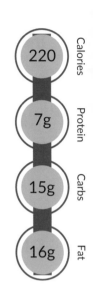

220 Calories

7g Protein

15g Carbs

16g Fat

INGREDIENTS

- 1 large cucumber, diced
- 2 large tomatoes, diced
- 1/4 cup red onion, thinly sliced
- 1/3 cup feta cheese, crumbled
- 10 black olives, pitted and halved
- 2 tablespoons olive oil
- 1 tablespoon red wine vinegar
- Salt and pepper to taste
- Fresh oregano or parsley, chopped (for garnish)

DIRECTIONS:

1. In a large bowl, mix together cucumber, tomatoes, and red onion.
2. Stir in feta cheese and olives.
3. Drizzle with olive oil and red wine vinegar. Season with salt and pepper.
4. Sprinkle with fresh oregano or parsley and serve immediately.

ROASTED BUTTERNUT SQUASH AND SAGE SOUP

⏱ 15 Mins	⧖ 0 Mins	👥 Serves: 2

180 Calories

4g Protein

28g Carbs

7g Fat

INGREDIENTS

- 1 medium butternut squash, peeled, seeded, and cubed
- 1 tablespoon olive oil
- 4 cups low-sodium vegetable broth
- 1 onion, chopped
- 2 cloves garlic, minced
- 6 fresh sage leaves, minced
- Salt and pepper to taste

DIRECTIONS:

1. Toss butternut squash with olive oil, salt, and pepper. Spread on a baking sheet and roast at 400°F (200°C) for 30 minutes until tender and lightly caramelized.
2. In a large pot, sauté onion and garlic in a splash of olive oil until translucent.
3. Add roasted squash, vegetable broth, and sage to the pot. Bring to a simmer and cook for 15 minutes.
4. Puree the soup with an immersion blender until smooth.
5. Season to taste, serve hot with a dollop of sour cream or Greek yogurt if desired.

BEETROOT AND ORANGE SALAD WITH WALNUTS

⏰ 15 Mins   ⏳ 0 Mins   👥 Serves: 2

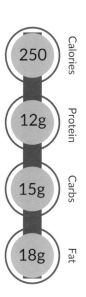

250 Calories

12g Protein

15g Carbs

18g Fat

INGREDIENTS

- 2 medium beetroots, cooked and sliced
- 2 oranges, peeled and segments removed
- 1/4 cup walnuts, roughly chopped
- 2 tablespoons olive oil
- 1 tablespoon balsamic vinegar
- Salt and pepper to taste
- Fresh mint leaves for garnish

DIRECTIONS:

1. Arrange sliced beetroots and orange segments on a serving plate.
2. In a small bowl, whisk together olive oil, balsamic vinegar, salt, and pepper.
3. Drizzle dressing over beetroots and oranges. Sprinkle with chopped walnuts.
4. Add fresh mint leaves as garnish before serving.

ROASTED RED PEPPER AND TOMATO SOUP

⏰ 10 Mins   ⏳ 20 Mins   👥 Serves: 2

180 Calories

4g Protein

27g Carbs

7g Fat

INGREDIENTS

- 2 large red bell peppers
- 3 medium tomatoes, quartered
- 1 small onion, chopped
- 2 cloves garlic, minced
- 2 cups vegetable broth
- 1 tablespoon olive oil
- 1/2 teaspoon smoked paprika
- Salt and freshly ground black pepper

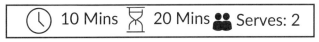

1. Preheat oven to 425°F (220°C). On a baking sheet, toss red peppers and tomatoes with olive oil, salt, and pepper. Roast for 20 minutes, turning once.
2. In a pot, sauté onion and garlic in olive oil until translucent.
3. After roasting, peel peppers, add to the pot with tomatoes, onion, and garlic. Add broth and simmer.
4. Blend the mixture until smooth with an immersion blender. Season with smoked paprika, salt, and pepper.
5. Serve the soup hot, garnished with fresh basil.

WHITE BEAN AND KALE SOUP

🕐 5 Mins ⧖ 20 Mins 👥 Serves: 2

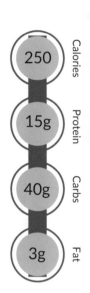

250 Calories
15g Protein
40g Carbs
3g Fat

- 1 can (15 oz) white beans, drained and rinsed
- 2 cups kale, chopped
- 1 medium onion, chopped
- 2 cloves garlic, minced
- 2 cups vegetable broth
- 1 teaspoon olive oil
- 1/2 teaspoon smoked paprika
- Salt and pepper to taste
- Optional: Parmesan cheese for garnish

DIRECTIONS:

1. In a pot, heat olive oil over medium heat. Add onion and garlic, cook until onion is translucent.
2. Stir in kale and cook until slightly wilted. Add white beans and stir to combine.
3. Pour in vegetable broth, bring to a simmer. Cook for about 15 minutes or until the kale is tender.
4. Add smoked paprika, salt, and pepper. Adjust seasoning to taste.
5. Ladle the soup into bowls. Garnish with Parmesan cheese if desired.

MEDITERRANEAN FISH SOUP

🕐 10 Mins ⧖ 20 Mins 👥 Serves: 2

220 Calories
23g Protein
12g Carbs
8g Fat

- 1/2 pound firm white fish fillets, such as cod or tilapia, cut into chunks
- 1 cup canned diced tomatoes
- 1 small onion, chopped
- 1 clove garlic, minced
- 1/2 cup chopped bell peppers
- 2 cups fish or vegetable broth
- 1/2 teaspoon dried oregano
- 1/2 teaspoon dried basil
- 1 tablespoon olive oil

1. In a pot, heat olive oil over medium heat. Add onion, garlic, and bell peppers; cook until softened, about 5 minutes.
2. Stir in the diced tomatoes and broth. Bring to a simmer.
3. Add oregano, basil, salt, and pepper.
4. Add the fish chunks to the pot. Simmer gently until the fish is cooked through, about 10-12 minutes.
5. Check seasoning, adjust if necessary. Serve hot, garnished with fresh parsley if using.

CAULIFLOWER AND TAHINI SOUP

 5 Mins ⏳ 25 Mins 👥 Serves: 2

- 1 medium head cauliflower, chopped into florets
- 2 tablespoons tahini (sesame seed paste)
- 1 small onion, chopped
- 2 cloves garlic, minced
- 3 cups vegetable broth
- 1 tablespoon olive oil
- 1 teaspoon cumin
- Salt and pepper to taste
- Optional: toasted sesame seeds for garnish

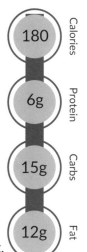

180 Calories
6g Protein
15g Carbs
12g Fat

1. In a large pot, heat olive oil over medium heat. Add onion and garlic, sauté until translucent, about 5 minutes.
2. Stir in cauliflower florets and cook for another 5 minutes until slightly softened.
3. Add vegetable broth to the pot and bring to a simmer. Cook until the cauliflower is very tender, about 15 minutes.
4. Using an immersion blender, puree the soup in the pot until smooth.
5. Mix in tahini and cumin. Season with salt and pepper to taste.
6. Serve hot, garnished with toasted sesame seeds if desired.

GREEK LEMON CHICKEN SOUP

 5 Mins 25 Mins 👥 Serves: 2

INGREDIENTS
- 1/2 pound chicken breast, cubed
- 3 cups chicken broth
- 1/4 cup orzo pasta or rice
- 2 eggs
- Juice of 1 large lemon
- 1 carrot, diced
- 1 stalk celery, diced
- 1 small onion, diced
- 1 tablespoon olive oil
- Salt and pepper to taste
- Optional: chopped fresh dill for garnish

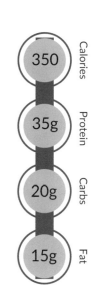

350 Calories
35g Protein
20g Carbs
15g Fat

DIRECTIONS:

1. In a pot, heat olive oil and sauté onion, carrot, and celery until softened.
2. Cook Chicken: Add chicken, cook until no longer pink.
3. Simmer: Add broth and orzo, simmer until pasta is tender.
4. Thicken Soup: Whisk eggs with lemon juice, temper with hot broth, then mix back into the soup.
5. Season with salt and pepper, heat briefly, and serve garnished with dill.

AVOCADO AND QUINOA SALAD

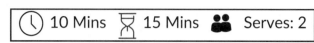

( ) 10 Mins ⧗ 15 Mins 👥 Serves: 2

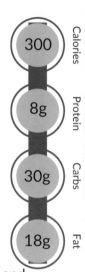

300 Calories
8g Protein
30g Carbs
18g Fat

INGREDIENTS

- 1/2 cup quinoa, rinsed
- 1 ripe avocado, diced
- 1/2 cup cherry tomatoes, halved
- 1/4 cup red onion, finely chopped
- 1/4 cup cucumber, diced
- 1/4 cup feta cheese, crumbled
- 2 tablespoons lemon juice
- 2 tablespoons olive oil
- Salt and pepper to taste

1. In a small saucepan, bring 1 cup of water to a boil. Add quinoa, reduce heat to low, cover, and simmer for 15 minutes or until water is absorbed. Fluff with a fork.
2. While quinoa cooks, prepare the avocado, tomatoes, onion, and cucumber.
3. In a large bowl, mix the cooked quinoa, avocado, tomatoes, onion, cucumber, and feta cheese.
4. Drizzle with lemon juice and olive oil. Toss to combine. Season with salt and pepper.
5. Garnish with fresh herbs if using and serve immediately or chilled.

BUTTERNUT SQUASH AND SAGE SOUP

( ) 10 Mins ⧗ 20 Mins 👥 Serves: 2

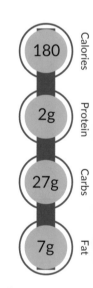

180 Calories
2g Protein
27g Carbs
7g Fat

INGREDIENTS

- 2 cups butternut squash, peeled and cubed
- 1 tablespoon fresh sage, chopped
- 1 small onion, chopped
- 2 cloves garlic, minced
- 2 cups vegetable broth
- 1 tablespoon olive oil
- Salt and pepper to taste
- Optional: dollop of cream or a sprinkle of roasted pumpkin seeds for garnish

DIRECTIONS:

1. In a large pot, heat olive oil over medium heat. Add onion and garlic, sauté until translucent.
2. Add butternut squash and sage to the pot, stir to combine with the aromatics.
3. Pour in vegetable broth, bring to a boil, then reduce heat and simmer until squash is tender, about 15 minutes.
4. Use an immersion blender to puree the soup directly in the pot until smooth.
5. Season with salt and pepper. Serve hot, garnished with cream or pumpkin seeds if desired.

Veggie

The "Veggie" chapter is dedicated to vegetable-focused recipes that highlight the versatility and health benefits of various vegetables. This section provides a range of dishes, from simple salads and steamed veggies to more complex stir-fries and roasted vegetable platters. Each recipe is designed to make vegetables the star of the meal, offering delicious, nutrient-packed options for any time of the day.

GARLIC SPINACH SAUTÉ

| 🕐 5 Mins | ⏳ 5 Mins | 👥 Serves: 2 |

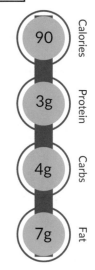

90 Calories
3g Protein
4g Carbs
7g Fat

INGREDIENTS

- 4 cups fresh spinach
- 2 cloves garlic, minced
- 1 tablespoon olive oil
- Salt and pepper to taste
- Lemon wedges for serving (optional)

DIRECTIONS:

1. In a large skillet, heat olive oil over medium heat.
2. Add garlic and sauté for about 1 minute until fragrant.
3. Add spinach to the skillet, seasoning with salt and pepper. Cook until spinach is wilted, about 3-4 minutes, stirring frequently.
4. Serve hot, with a squeeze of lemon if desired.

STUFFED BELL PEPPERS WITH QUINOA AND FETA

| 🕐 5 Mins | ⏳ 25 Mins | 👥 Serves: 2 |

290 Calories
9g Protein
35g Carbs
15g Fat

- 2 large bell peppers, halved and seeds removed
- 1/2 cup quinoa, cooked
- 1/4 cup feta cheese, crumbled
- 1/4 cup diced tomatoes
- 1/4 cup chopped spinach
- 1 small onion, finely chopped
- 1 clove garlic, minced
- 2 tablespoons olive oil
- Salt and pepper to taste

1. Preheat oven to 375°F (190°C).
2. In a skillet, heat 1 tablespoon olive oil over medium heat. Sauté onion and garlic until translucent. Add spinach and tomatoes, cook until spinach is wilted. Remove from heat, mix in cooked quinoa and feta cheese. Season with salt and pepper.
3. Fill each bell pepper half with the quinoa mixture.
4. Place stuffed peppers in a baking dish, drizzle with remaining olive oil, and bake for 20-25 minutes until peppers are tender.

GRILLED ZUCCHINI WITH LEMON AND HERBS

| 10 Mins | 8 Mins | Serves: 2 |

INGREDIENTS

- 2 medium zucchinis, sliced lengthwise
- 1 lemon, zested and juiced
- 2 tablespoons olive oil
- 1 tablespoon fresh herbs (such as thyme or basil), chopped
- Salt and pepper to taste

150 Calories
2g Protein
10g Carbs
10g Fat

DIRECTIONS:

1. Brush zucchini slices with olive oil and season with salt and pepper.
2. Preheat grill to medium-high heat. Grill zucchini slices for about 4 minutes per side or until tender and grill marks appear.
3. Mix lemon zest, lemon juice, and chopped herbs in a small bowl.
4. Drizzle lemon and herb mixture over grilled zucchini and serve immediately.

BAKED RATATOUILLE WITH CRISPY CHICKPEA TOPPING

| 10 Mins | 20 Mins | Serves: 2 |

- 1 small zucchini, sliced
- 1 small eggplant, sliced
- 1 red bell pepper, sliced
- 1 small onion, sliced
- 1 cup canned chickpeas, drained and rinsed
- 2 tablespoons olive oil
- 1 teaspoon dried thyme
- 1/2 cup tomato sauce
- Salt and pepper to taste
- Optional: fresh basil for garnish

290 Calories
9g Protein
35g Carbs
15g Fat

1. Toss zucchini, eggplant, bell pepper, and onion with 1 tablespoon olive oil, salt, and pepper. Arrange in a baking dish.
2. Toss chickpeas with remaining olive oil and thyme. Spread on a baking sheet.
3. Place both the vegetable dish and chickpeas in a preheated 425°F (220°C) oven. Bake for 20 minutes, or until vegetables are tender and chickpeas are crispy.
4. Spoon tomato sauce over the roasted vegetables and top with crispy chickpeas.
5. Garnish with fresh basil if desired.

EGGPLANT PARMESAN STACKS

⏰ 20 Mins ⏳ 30 Mins 👥 Serves: 2

INGREDIENTS
- 1 large eggplant, sliced into 1/2-inch rounds
- 1 cup low-sodium marinara sauce
- 1/2 cup shredded mozzarella cheese (low-fat)
- 1/4 cup grated Parmesan cheese
- 1/4 cup breadcrumbs (optional for texture)
- 2 tablespoons olive oil
- 1 teaspoon dried basil
- Salt and pepper to taste
- Fresh basil leaves for garnish

350 Calories
15g Protein
30g Carbs
20g Fat

DIRECTIONS:
1. Salt eggplant slices, rest for 10 minutes, then pat dry.
2. Brush slices with olive oil, bake at 375°F for 20 minutes, flipping once.
3. Layer eggplant, marinara, mozzarella, and Parmesan on a baking sheet. Repeat layers, top with breadcrumbs if desired.
4. Bake for another 10 minutes until cheese is bubbly.
5. Garnish with fresh basil and serve immediately.

EGGPLANT AND ZUCCHINI LAYER CAKE WITH GOAT CHEESE FROSTING

⏰ 20 Mins ⏳ 30 Mins 👥 Serves: 2

- 1 medium eggplant, sliced into 1/4-inch rounds
- 1 medium zucchini, sliced into 1/4-inch rounds
- 4 oz goat cheese, softened
- 2 tablespoons olive oil
- 1 teaspoon dried thyme
- Salt and pepper to taste
- Fresh basil for garnish

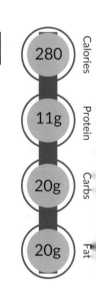
280 Calories
11g Protein
20g Carbs
20g Fat

1. Brush eggplant and zucchini with olive oil, season, and roast at 375°F for 20 minutes, turning once.
2. Prepare Goat Cheese: Whip goat cheese, adding olive oil as needed for smoothness.
3. Assemble Cake: Layer roasted vegetables and goat cheese alternately to form a cake.
4. Set Cake: Chill for 10 minutes to firm up the layers before serving.

SPICY STUFFED ZUCCHINI BOATS

⏱ 10 Mins ⏳ 20 Mins 👥 Serves: 2

- 2 medium zucchinis, halved lengthwise and hollowed out
- 1/2 cup cooked quinoa
- 1/4 cup bell peppers, finely diced
- 1/4 cup black beans, rinsed and drained
- 1/4 cup corn kernels
- 1 small onion, diced
- 2 cloves garlic, minced
- 1 teaspoon chili powder
- 1/2 teaspoon cumin
- 2 tablespoons olive oil
- Salt and pepper to taste

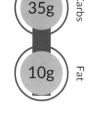
250 Calories
8g Protein
35g Carbs
10g Fat

DIRECTIONS:

1. Hollow out each zucchini half to form boats.
2. In a skillet, cook onion, garlic, bell peppers, and spices until soft.
3. Combine the sautéed veggies with quinoa, black beans, and corn. Season to taste.
4. Fill the zucchini boats with the vegetable mixture.
5. Place on a baking sheet and bake at 375°F for 20 minutes.
6. Top with fresh cilantro and serve warm.

GREEK STYLE GREEN BEANS WITH TOMATO AND FETA

⏱ 10 Mins ⏳ 20 Mins 👥 Serves: 2

- 2 cups green beans, trimmed
- 1 cup diced tomatoes
- 1/2 onion, sliced
- 2 cloves garlic, minced
- 1/4 cup crumbled feta cheese
- 2 tablespoons olive oil
- 1 teaspoon dried oregano
- Salt and pepper to taste
- Fresh parsley for garnish

200 Calories
6g Protein
18g Carbs
12g Fat

DIRECTIONS:

1. In a skillet, heat olive oil over medium heat. Add onions and garlic, cooking until softened.
2. Stir in green beans and tomatoes, season with oregano, salt, and pepper. Cover and simmer for about 15 minutes, or until beans are tender.
3. Sprinkle feta cheese over the beans and cook for an additional 5 minutes.
4. Garnish with fresh parsley and serve warm.

MEDITERRANEAN GRILLED VEGETABLE PLATTER

| ⏰ 10 Mins | ⏳ 20 Mins | 👥 Serves: 2 |

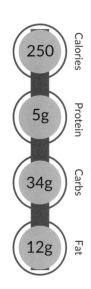

Calories 250
Protein 5g
Carbs 34g
Fat 12g

- 1 zucchini, sliced into rounds
- 1 bell pepper, cut into strips
- 1 eggplant, sliced into rounds
- 1 red onion, cut into wedges
- 2 tablespoons olive oil
- Salt and pepper to taste
- 1 teaspoon dried oregano
- 1 teaspoon dried basil
- Optional: balsamic vinegar, for drizzling

1. Heat your grill to medium-high.
2. Toss zucchini, bell pepper, eggplant, and onion with olive oil, salt, pepper, oregano, and basil in a large bowl.
3. Place vegetables on the grill and cook for about 10 minutes on each side, until tender and charred.
4. Arrange grilled vegetables on a platter. Drizzle with balsamic vinegar if desired, and serve immediately.

HERB-ROASTED ARTICHOKES

| ⏰ 10 Mins | ⏳ 20 Mins | 👥 Serves: 2 |

Calories 190
Protein 4g
Carbs 15g
Fat 14g

- 2 whole artichokes
- 2 tablespoons olive oil
- 2 cloves garlic, minced
- 1 lemon, halved
- 1 teaspoon dried thyme
- 1 teaspoon dried rosemary
- Salt and pepper to taste

DIRECTIONS:

1. Rinse and trim artichokes, removing top third and tough leaves. Halve vertically, remove chokes.
2. Preheat Oven: Set to 400°F (200°C).
3. Season: Rub with lemon, oil, and season with garlic, thyme, rosemary, salt, and pepper.
4. Roast: Place cut-side down on a parchment-lined baking sheet. Roast for 20 minutes or until tender.
5. Serve: Finish with a squeeze of fresh lemon juice.

GARLIC SPINACH AND MUSHROOM SAUTÉ

5 Mins   10 Mins   Serves: 2

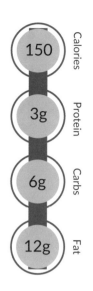

150 Calories
3g Protein
6g Carbs
12g Fat

INGREDIENTS

- 2 cups fresh spinach
- 1 cup sliced mushrooms
- 2 cloves garlic, minced
- 2 tablespoons olive oil
- Salt and pepper to taste
- Optional: A sprinkle of grated Parmesan cheese

DIRECTIONS:

1. In a large skillet, heat olive oil over medium heat.
2. Add garlic and mushrooms to the skillet. Sauté for about 5 minutes until the mushrooms are golden and softened.
3. Stir in the spinach and cook until wilted, about 2-3 minutes. Season with salt and pepper.
4. Serve hot, optionally sprinkled with Parmesan cheese.

TOMATO AND BASIL ZUCCHINI NOODLES

10 Mins   5 Mins   Serves: 2

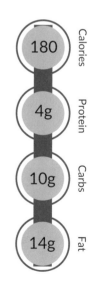

180 Calories
4g Protein
10g Carbs
14g Fat

INGREDIENTS

- 2 large zucchinis, spiralized
- 1 cup cherry tomatoes, halved
- 2 cloves garlic, minced
- 1/4 cup fresh basil leaves, chopped
- 2 tablespoons olive oil
- Salt and pepper to taste
- Optional: Grated Parmesan cheese for topping

1. Spiralize the zucchinis and set aside.
2. Heat olive oil in a large skillet over medium heat. Add garlic and tomatoes, sautéing until tomatoes are just soft, about 2-3 minutes.
3. Stir in the zucchini noodles and cook for about 2 minutes, until just tender.
4. Add fresh basil, salt, and pepper, tossing to combine well.
5. Dish out the noodles and top with grated Parmesan if desired.

CARAMELIZED ONION AND FETA TART

 10 Mins | 20 Mins | Serves: 2

INGREDIENTS

- 1 large onion, thinly sliced
- 1 tablespoon olive oil
- 1 tablespoon balsamic vinegar
- 1 pre-made pie crust or puff pastry sheet
- 1/2 cup feta cheese, crumbled
- Salt and pepper to taste
- Fresh thyme leaves for garnish

320 Calories
7g Protein
34g Carbs
18g Fat

1. In a skillet over medium heat, heat olive oil. Add sliced onions and a pinch of salt. Cook, stirring occasionally, until onions are golden and caramelized, about 15 minutes. Near the end, add balsamic vinegar and stir to combine.
2. Roll out the pie crust or puff pastry into a small tart pan or baking sheet.
3. Spread the caramelized onions evenly over the crust. Sprinkle crumbled feta cheese on top.
4. Preheat oven to 375°F (190°C). Bake the tart for about 20 minutes or until the edges are golden brown and the cheese is slightly melted.
5. Remove from oven, sprinkle with fresh thyme, slice, and serve.

ROASTED CAULIFLOWER WITH TAHINI SAUCE

10 Mins | 20 Mins | Serves: 2

INGREDIENTS

- 1 large head of cauliflower, cut into florets
- 2 tablespoons olive oil
- Salt and pepper to taste
- 1/4 cup tahini
- 2 tablespoons lemon juice
- 1 garlic clove, minced
- 2-3 tablespoons water (to thin sauce)
- 1 tablespoon chopped parsley (for garnish)

DIRECTIONS:

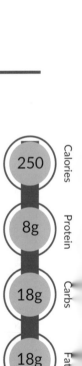

250 Calories
8g Protein
18g Carbs
18g Fat

1. Toss cauliflower florets with olive oil, salt, and pepper. Spread on a baking sheet.
2. Preheat oven to 425°F (220°C). Roast cauliflower for 20 minutes, or until tender and edges are golden brown.
3. While the cauliflower roasts, whisk together tahini, lemon juice, minced garlic, and water in a bowl until smooth.
4. Drizzle tahini sauce over the roasted cauliflower. Garnish with chopped parsley.

GREEK STYLE ROASTED POTATOES

🕐 10 Mins ⏳ 20 Mins 👥 Serves: 2

- 4 large potatoes, peeled and cut into chunks
- 2 tablespoons olive oil
- 1 teaspoon dried oregano
- 1/2 teaspoon garlic powder
- Salt and freshly ground black pepper, to taste
- 1/2 lemon, juiced
- Fresh parsley, chopped (for garnish)

250	Calories
5g	Protein
45g	Carbs
7g	Fat

DIRECTIONS:

1. Preheat your oven to 425°F (220°C).
2. Toss the potato chunks with olive oil, oregano, garlic powder, salt, and pepper until well coated.
3. Spread the potatoes in a single layer on a baking sheet. Roast for 20 minutes, or until golden and crispy, turning halfway through.
4. Remove from the oven and immediately drizzle with fresh lemon juice.
5. Garnish with chopped parsley before serving.

ASPARAGUS AND LEMON RISOTTO

🕐 5 Mins ⏳ 25 Mins 👥 Serves: 2

- 1 cup Arborio rice
- 2 cups low-sodium vegetable broth
- 1 bunch asparagus, trimmed and cut into 1-inch pieces
- 1 small onion, finely chopped
- 2 cloves garlic, minced
- 2 tablespoons olive oil
- Zest and juice of 1 lemon
- 1/4 cup grated Parmesan cheese

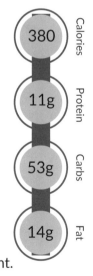

380	Calories
11g	Protein
53g	Carbs
14g	Fat

1. In a large pan, heat olive oil over medium heat. Add onion and garlic, sauté until translucent.
2. Add Arborio rice, stirring to coat with oil. Toast the rice for about 2 minutes.
3. Gradually add vegetable broth, a half cup at a time, stirring frequently. Wait until each addition is almost fully absorbed before adding the next.
4. Halfway through cooking, add the asparagus.
5. Once the rice is tender and creamy, stir in lemon zest, lemon juice, and Parmesan cheese. Season with salt and pepper to taste.

BAKED GARLIC PARMESAN ZUCCHINI CHIPS

🕐 10 Mins ⏳ 20 Mins 👥 Serves: 2

INGREDIENTS

- 2 medium zucchini, thinly sliced
- 1/4 cup grated Parmesan cheese
- 1/4 teaspoon garlic powder
- 1 tablespoon olive oil
- Salt and pepper, to taste

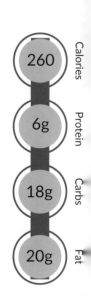

120 Calories

5g Protein

8g Carbs

8g Fat

DIRECTIONS:

1. Preheat the oven to 425°F (220°C). Line a baking sheet with parchment paper.
2. In a bowl, toss the zucchini slices with olive oil, garlic powder, salt, and pepper.
3. Arrange the zucchini slices in a single layer on the prepared baking sheet.
4. Sprinkle grated Parmesan cheese over the zucchini slices.
5. Bake in the preheated oven for 20 minutes, or until crispy and golden brown.
6. Serve immediately, additional Parmesan sprinkled on top if desired.

CHARGRILLED VEGETABLES WITH ROMESCO SAUCE

🕐 10 Mins ⏳ 15 Mins 👥 Serves: 2

- 1 red bell pepper, quartered
- 1 yellow bell pepper, quartered
- 1 zucchini, sliced lengthwise
- 1 eggplant, sliced lengthwise
- 1 tablespoon olive oil

For the Romesco Sauce:
- 1/2 cup roasted red peppers
- 1/4 cup almonds, toasted
- 1 garlic clove
- 2 tablespoons tomato paste
- 2 tablespoons red wine vinegar
- 1/4 cup olive oil
- Salt and chili flakes, to taste

260 Calories

6g Protein

18g Carbs

20g Fat

1. Preheat grill to medium-high heat.
2. Brush vegetables with olive oil and season with salt and pepper.
3. Grill vegetables for about 6-8 minutes per side or until charred and tender.
4. For the sauce, blend roasted red peppers, almonds, garlic, tomato paste, vinegar, and olive oil in a blender until smooth. Season with salt and chili flakes.
5. Serve grilled vegetables with a dollop of romesco sauce on top.

Meat

ROAST CHICKEN WITH MEDITERRANEAN HERB STUFFING

⏱ 10 Mins	⏳ 20 Mins	👥 Serves: 2

- 2 large chicken breasts, boneless and skinless
- 1 cup fresh breadcrumbs
- 1/4 cup chopped fresh herbs (parsley, thyme, rosemary)
- 1 garlic clove, minced
- 2 tablespoons olive oil
- 1/4 cup chopped onions
- 1/4 cup diced bell peppers
- Salt and pepper, to taste
- Lemon wedges, for serving

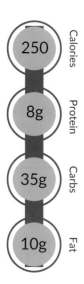

250 Calories
8g Protein
35g Carbs
10g Fat

DIRECTIONS:

1. Heat oven to 375°F (190°C). Warm olive oil in a pan, sauté onions and bell peppers until soft.
2. Combine breadcrumbs, veggies, herbs, garlic, salt, and pepper in a bowl.
3. Make a pocket in each chicken breast, stuff with the breadcrumb mix.
4. Arrange chicken on a tray, drizzle with olive oil, and season.
5. Roast for 20 minutes until fully cooked.
6. Serve hot with lemon wedges.

SIMPLE BEEF KOFTAS

⏱ 10 Mins	⏳ 10 Mins	👥 Serves: 2

INGREDIENTS

- 1/2 pound ground beef (85% lean)
- 1 small onion, finely chopped
- 2 cloves garlic, minced
- 2 tablespoons fresh parsley, chopped
- 1 teaspoon ground cumin
- 1/2 teaspoon ground coriander
- 1/4 teaspoon ground cinnamon
- 1/4 teaspoon cayenne pepper
- Salt and black pepper, to taste
- Olive oil, for grilling

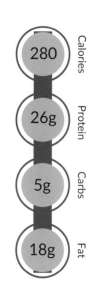

280 Calories
26g Protein
5g Carbs
18g Fat

1. In a mixing bowl, combine ground beef, onion, garlic, parsley, cumin, coriander, cinnamon, cayenne pepper, salt, and black pepper. Mix until well combined.
2. Divide the mixture into 4 equal parts and shape each into a long, thin kofta around skewers.
3. Preheat a grill or grill pan to medium-high heat and lightly oil the grates.
4. Grill the koftas for about 4-5 minutes on each side or until fully cooked and nicely charred.
5. Serve hot, optionally with pita bread, yogurt sauce, or a fresh salad.

TURKISH MEATBALLS IN TOMATO SAUCE

🕐 10 Mins ⧗ 20 Mins 👥 Serves: 2

- 1/2 lb ground beef
- 1/4 cup breadcrumbs
- 1 egg
- 1 small onion, finely chopped
- 2 cloves garlic, minced
- 1/2 tsp cumin
- 1/2 tsp paprika
- Salt and pepper to taste
- 1 tbsp olive oil
- 1 cup tomato sauce
- Fresh parsley, chopped for garnish

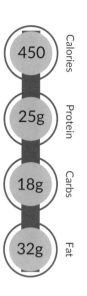

Calories 450
Protein 25g
Carbs 18g
Fat 32g

DIRECTIONS:

1. Mix beef, breadcrumbs, egg, onion, half the garlic, cumin, paprika, salt, and pepper in a bowl.
2. Form into small meatballs.
3. Heat olive oil in a skillet, brown meatballs on all sides.
4. Add remaining garlic to the skillet, sauté briefly.
5. Pour tomato sauce over meatballs, simmer for 15 minutes.
6. Garnish with parsley and serve.

PORK TENDERLOIN WITH ROSEMARY AND GARLIC

🕐 10 Mins ⧗ 25 Mins 👥 Serves: 2

INGREDIENTS

- 1 pound pork tenderloin
- 3 cloves garlic, minced
- 2 tablespoons fresh rosemary, chopped
- 2 tablespoons olive oil
- Salt and pepper to taste

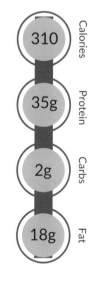

Calories 310
Protein 35g
Carbs 2g
Fat 18g

DIRECTIONS:

1. Rub pork tenderloin with olive oil, garlic, rosemary, salt, and pepper.
2. Preheat oven to 375°F (190°C). Place the seasoned tenderloin on a roasting pan.
3. Roast in the oven for 25 minutes or until the internal temperature reaches 145°F (63°C).
4. Let the pork rest for 5 minutes before slicing.

ITALIAN SAUSAGE AND PEPPER SKILLET

 10 Mins ⧗ 20 Mins 👥 Serves: 2

INGREDIENTS

- 2 Italian sausages (choose low-sodium, if available)
- 1 red bell pepper, sliced
- 1 green bell pepper, sliced
- 1 onion, sliced
- 2 cloves garlic, minced
- 1 tablespoon olive oil
- 1 teaspoon dried oregano
- Salt and pepper to taste

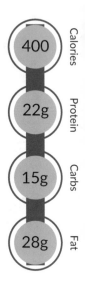

400 Calories
22g Protein
15g Carbs
28g Fat

1. In a skillet over medium heat, brown the sausages until cooked through, about 10 minutes. Remove and slice.
2. In the same skillet, add olive oil, peppers, onion, and garlic. Cook until vegetables are tender, about 8 minutes.
3. Return sliced sausages to the skillet. Sprinkle with oregano, salt, and pepper, stirring to combine.
4. Cook for an additional 2 minutes to blend flavors and serve hot.

GARLIC LEMON CHICKEN SKEWERS

🕐 10 Mins ⧗ 15 Mins 👥 Serves: 2

INGREDIENTS

- 1 pound chicken breast, cut into cubes
- 3 cloves garlic, minced
- Zest and juice of 1 lemon
- 2 tablespoons olive oil
- 1 teaspoon dried thyme
- Salt and pepper to taste
- Wooden or metal skewers

310 Calories
35g Protein
2g Carbs
18g Fat

DIRECTIONS:

1. Mix lemon zest, juice, garlic, olive oil, thyme, salt, and pepper in a bowl. Add chicken and marinate for 30 minutes in the fridge.
2. Soak wooden skewers in water for 30 minutes to avoid burning.
3. Evenly skewer the marinated chicken cubes.
4. Heat grill to medium-high. Grill skewers about 5 minutes per side until cooked and charred.
5. Serve hot with extra lemon wedges

ONE-PAN MEDITERRANEAN CHICKEN WITH OLIVES AND TOMATOES

 10 Mins  20 Mins 👥 Serves: 2

INGREDIENTS

- 2 chicken breasts, boneless and skinless
- 1 cup cherry tomatoes, halved
- 1/2 cup pitted Kalamata olives
- 1 onion, sliced
- 2 cloves garlic, minced
- 2 tablespoons olive oil
- 1 teaspoon dried oregano
- Salt and pepper to taste
- Fresh basil for garnish

320 Calories
28g Protein
12g Carbs
18g Fat

1. Season chicken with salt, pepper, and oregano.
2. In a large skillet, heat olive oil over medium heat. Add chicken and cook until golden on both sides, about 5 minutes per side.
3. To the skillet, add onions, garlic, tomatoes, and olives. Cook for an additional 10 minutes until the chicken is cooked through and vegetables are softened.
4. Garnish with fresh basil and serve hot

SPANISH MEATBALLS WITH SHERRY TOMATO SAUCE

 15 Mins  30 Mins 👥 Serves: 2

INGREDIENTS

- 1/2 pound ground beef
- 1/4 cup breadcrumbs
- 1 egg
- 1 garlic clove, minced
- 1/2 teaspoon smoked paprika
- 1/4 teaspoon cumin
- 1 cup canned tomatoes, crushed
- 1/4 cup sherry
- 1 onion, finely chopped
- 2 tablespoons olive oil
- Salt and pepper to taste
- Fresh parsley, chopped for garnish

450 Calories
28g Protein
20g Carbs
28g Fat

DIRECTIONS:

1. Combine beef, breadcrumbs, egg, spices, and season. Form into meatballs.
2. Brown in skillet with olive oil, remove.
3. Cook onion in same skillet, add sherry, reduce. Add tomatoes, simmer.
4. Return meatballs to skillet, cover, simmer 20 minutes. Garnish with parsley.

HERB-INFUSED LAMB CHOPS

🕙 10 Mins ⏳ 15 Mins 👥 Serves: 2

INGREDIENTS

- 4 lamb chops, about 1 inch thick
- 2 tablespoons olive oil
- 2 cloves garlic, minced
- 1 tablespoon fresh rosemary, chopped
- 1 tablespoon fresh thyme, chopped
- Salt and pepper to taste
- Lemon wedges, for serving

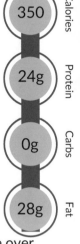
350 Calories
24g Protein
0g Carbs
28g Fat

1. In a small bowl, combine olive oil, garlic, rosemary, thyme, salt, and pepper. Rub the mixture over the lamb chops and let them marinate for at least 15 minutes at room temperature.
2. Heat a grill or grill pan over medium-high heat.
3. Place the lamb chops on the hot grill and cook for about 6-7 minutes on each side for medium-rare, or until desired doneness.
4. Let the lamb chops rest for a few minutes after grilling. Serve with lemon wedges to squeeze over the chops.

BALSAMIC GLAZED BEEF SKEWERS

🕙 15 Mins ⏳ 10 Mins 👥 Serves: 2

INGREDIENTS

- 1/2 pound beef sirloin, cut into 1-inch cubes
- 1/4 cup balsamic vinegar
- 2 tablespoons olive oil
- 2 cloves garlic, minced
- 1 teaspoon dried rosemary
- 1 teaspoon dried thyme
- Salt and pepper to taste
- 1 red bell pepper, cut into 1-inch pieces
- 1 onion, cut into 1-inch pieces

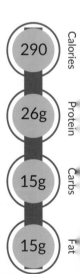
290 Calories
26g Protein
15g Carbs
15g Fat

1. In a bowl, whisk together balsamic vinegar, olive oil, garlic, rosemary, thyme, salt, and pepper. Add beef cubes and toss to coat. Marinate for at least 10 minutes.
2. Thread the marinated beef, bell pepper, and onion onto skewers.
3. Heat a grill or grill pan over medium-high heat.
4. Place the skewers on the grill and cook for about 5 minutes on each side or until beef reaches desired doneness.
5. Remove from grill and serve immediately.

CHICKEN PICCATA WITH CAPERS

🕐 10 Mins ⏳ 20 Mins 👥 Serves: 2

- 2 boneless, skinless chicken breasts, pounded to even thickness
- 1/4 cup all-purpose flour
- Salt and pepper to taste
- 2 tablespoons olive oil
- 1/4 cup fresh lemon juice
- 1/2 cup chicken broth
- 1/4 cup capers, rinsed
- 2 tablespoons unsalted butter
- Fresh parsley, chopped, for garnish

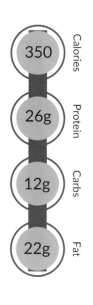

Calories 350
Protein 26g
Carbs 12g
Fat 22g

1. Season chicken breasts with salt and pepper, then dredge in flour, shaking off excess.
2. In a skillet, heat olive oil over medium-high heat. Add chicken and cook until golden and cooked through, about 4-5 minutes per side. Remove chicken from skillet and set aside.
3. In the same skillet, add lemon juice, chicken broth, and capers. Bring to a boil, scraping up any browned bits from the pan.
4. Reduce heat to low and stir in butter until melted. Return chicken to the skillet and simmer for a couple of minutes to reheat and coat with sauce.
5. Plate chicken and spoon over the sauce. Garnish with chopped parsley.

SPICED MOROCCAN CHICKEN

🕐 10 Mins ⏳ 20 Mins 👥 Serves: 2

- 2 chicken breasts
- 1 tsp ground cumin
- 1 tsp ground coriander
- 1/2 tsp ground cinnamon
- 1/2 tsp paprika
- Salt and pepper to taste
- 2 tbsp olive oil
- 1/2 cup chicken broth
- 1 tbsp honey
- 2 tbsp lemon juice
- Fresh cilantro, chopped, for garnish

Calories 295
Protein 26g
Carbs 9g
Fat 16g

1. Mix cumin, coriander, cinnamon, paprika, salt, and pepper. Rub this spice mix all over the chicken breasts.
2. Heat olive oil in a skillet over medium heat. Add chicken and cook until browned on both sides, about 5-6 minutes per side.
3. Add chicken broth, honey, and lemon juice to the skillet, bringing to a simmer. Cover and cook for another 10 minutes, or until the chicken is cooked through.
4. Garnish with chopped cilantro and serve hot.

GRILLED HARISSA LAMB RIBS

🕐 15 Mins ⏳ 25 Mins 👥 Serves: 2

INGREDIENTS

- 1 lb lamb ribs
- 2 tbsp harissa paste
- 1 tbsp olive oil
- 2 cloves garlic, minced
- 1 tsp ground cumin
- Salt and pepper to taste
- Fresh mint, chopped, for garnish

580 Calories

24g Protein

2g Carbs

50g Fat

DIRECTIONS:

1. In a bowl, combine harissa paste, olive oil, garlic, cumin, salt, and pepper. Rub this mixture all over the lamb ribs. Let marinate for at least 30 minutes, or overnight for best results.
2. Heat your grill to medium-high.
3. Place the ribs on the grill. Cook for about 10-12 minutes on each side, or until they reach your desired level of doneness.
4. Let the ribs rest for a few minutes after grilling. Garnish with chopped mint before serving.

LAMB KEBABS WITH YOGURT SAUCE

🕐 15 Mins ⏳ 10 Mins 👥 Serves: 2

INGREDIENTS

- 1 lb lamb, cut into 1-inch cubes
- 2 tablespoons olive oil
- 1 teaspoon paprika
- 1 teaspoon cumin
- 1/2 teaspoon coriander
- Salt and pepper to taste
- 1 cup Greek yogurt
- 1 tablespoon lemon juice
- 1 garlic clove, minced
- 1 tablespoon fresh mint, finely chopped
- Wooden or metal skewers

450 Calories

28g Protein

20g Carbs

28g Fat

DIRECTIONS:

1. Combine lamb cubes with olive oil, spices, and seasoning. Chill for 30 minutes.
2. Mix yogurt, lemon juice, garlic, and mint. Refrigerate.
3. Thread lamb on skewers.
4. Cook on medium-high for 10 minutes, turning for even browning.
5. Enjoy hot with yogurt sauce.

MEDITERRANEAN CHICKEN PITA POCKETS

⏰ 15 Mins ⏳ 10 Mins 👥 Serves: 2

- 2 whole wheat pita breads
- 1 chicken breast, grilled and sliced
- 1/2 cup mixed salad greens
- 1/4 cup cherry tomatoes, halved
- 1/4 cucumber, sliced
- 1/4 red onion, thinly sliced
- 2 tablespoons tzatziki sauce
- 2 tablespoons feta cheese, crumbled
- 1 tablespoon olives, sliced
- 1 teaspoon olive oil

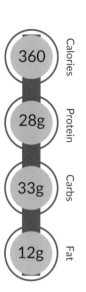
360 Calories
28g Protein
33g Carbs
12g Fat

1. Slice the grilled chicken breast. Prepare the vegetables and set aside.
2. Cut pita breads in half to make pockets. Open gently and spread tzatziki sauce inside each half.
3. Layer chicken slices, salad greens, tomatoes, cucumber slices, red onion, and olives inside the pita pockets. Sprinkle with feta cheese.
4. Drizzle a bit of olive oil over the filling in each pocket. Add salt and pepper to taste.
5. Serve the pita pockets immediately, or wrap them up for a quick and nutritious meal on the go.

MEDITERRANEAN STUFFED BEEF ROLLS

⏰ 15 Mins ⏳ 15 Mins 👥 Serves: 2

INGREDIENTS

- 4 thin beef steak slices (about 1/2 pound)
- 1/4 cup spinach, chopped
- 2 tablespoons feta cheese, crumbled
- 1/4 cup roasted red peppers, sliced
- 1 tablespoon fresh basil, chopped
- 1 clove garlic, minced
- Salt and pepper to taste
- 1 tablespoon olive oil

300 Calories
25g Protein
4g Carbs
20g Fat

DIRECTIONS:

1. Lay beef slices flat on a work surface. Season with salt and pepper.
2. Evenly distribute spinach, feta cheese, roasted red peppers, and basil on each beef slice.
3. Carefully roll each slice up over the filling, securing with a toothpick if necessary.
4. Heat olive oil in a skillet over medium heat. Add garlic and cook for 1 minute. Place beef rolls in the skillet, seam side down. Cook for about 3-4 minutes per side or until the beef is browned and cooked to desired doneness.
5. Remove toothpicks, slice if desired, and serve hot.

GREEK-STYLE GRILLED RIBEYE

⏲ 10 Mins ⧖ 10 Mins 👥 Serves: 2

INGREDIENTS

- 2 ribeye steaks (about 1 inch thick)
- 2 tablespoons olive oil
- 1 tablespoon fresh lemon juice
- 2 cloves garlic, minced
- 1 teaspoon dried oregano
- Salt and pepper to taste
- Fresh parsley, chopped (for garnish)

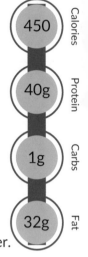

450 Calories
40g Protein
1g Carbs
32g Fat

1. In a small bowl, whisk together olive oil, lemon juice, minced garlic, oregano, salt, and pepper. Place ribeye steaks in a shallow dish and pour marinade over them. Ensure both sides are well coated. Let marinate for at least 30 minutes at room temperature.
2. Heat grill to high. Once hot, brush the grill grate with oil to prevent sticking.
3. Place the steaks on the grill and cook for 4-5 minutes on each side for medium-rare, or longer depending on desired doneness.
4. Let steaks rest for 5 minutes after grilling to allow juices to redistribute. Garnish with chopped parsley before serving.

PAPRIKA-RUBBED CHICKEN THIGHS

⏲ 10 Mins ⧖ 20 Mins 👥 Serves: 2

INGREDIENTS

- 4 chicken thighs, bone-in, skin-on
- 2 tablespoons olive oil
- 2 teaspoons smoked paprika
- 1 teaspoon garlic powder
- 1/2 teaspoon onion powder
- Salt and pepper to taste
- Fresh herbs (like parsley or cilantro) for garnish

300 Calories
25g Protein
1g Carbs
22g Fat

DIRECTIONS:

1. Preheat your oven to 400°F (200°C).
2. Season chicken thighs with smoked paprika, garlic powder, onion powder, salt, pepper, and olive oil.
3. Arrange on a baking sheet skin-side up.
4. Bake for 20 minutes until crispy and cooked through. Let rest, garnish with herbs, and serve.

ITALIAN HERBED MEATBALLS IN MARINARA

🕐 15 Mins　⧗ 20 Mins　👥 Serves: 2

- 1/2 pound ground beef
- 1/4 cup breadcrumbs
- 1 large egg
- 2 cloves garlic, minced
- 1 tablespoon chopped fresh basil
- 1 tablespoon chopped fresh parsley
- 1/4 teaspoon salt
- 1/4 teaspoon black pepper
- 1 cup marinara sauce
- 1 tablespoon olive oil

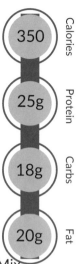

350 Calories
25g Protein
18g Carbs
20g Fat

1. In a bowl, combine ground beef, breadcrumbs, egg, garlic, basil, parsley, salt, and pepper. Mix well.
2. Shape the mixture into 1-inch meatballs.
3. Heat olive oil in a skillet over medium heat. Add meatballs and cook until browned on all sides.
4. Pour marinara sauce over meatballs, reduce heat to low, and simmer for 10 minutes until meatballs are cooked through.
5. Serve hot, garnished with additional basil or parsley if desired.

ZA'ATAR SPICED LAMB KEBABS

🕐 20 Mins　⧗ 10 Mins　👥 Serves: 2

INGREDIENTS

- 1 pound lamb, cut into 1-inch cubes
- 2 tablespoons za'atar seasoning
- 1 tablespoon olive oil
- 1 teaspoon salt
- 1/2 teaspoon black pepper
- 1 red onion, cut into chunks
- 1 bell pepper, cut into chunks
- Fresh parsley, chopped (for garnish)
- Lemon wedges (for serving)

480 Calories
45g Protein
12g Carbs
28g Fat

DIRECTIONS:

1. Mix lamb, za'atar, oil, salt, and pepper; marinate for 15 mins.
2. Soak skewers if wooden.
3. Thread lamb, onion, and bell pepper.
4. Grill on medium-high, 8-10 mins. Serve with parsley and lemon.

SUMAC-SPICED PORK CHOPS

 10 Mins 15 Mins Serves: 2

INGREDIENTS

- 2 pork chops, bone-in
- 1 tablespoon sumac
- 1 teaspoon smoked paprika
- 1/2 teaspoon garlic powder
- Salt and pepper, to taste
- 2 tablespoons olive oil
- Fresh parsley, chopped (for garnish)
- Lemon wedges (for serving)

320	Calories
29g	Protein
2g	Carbs
22g	Fat

1. In a small bowl, mix sumac, smoked paprika, garlic powder, salt, and pepper.
2. Rub the spice mixture evenly over both sides of the pork chops.
3. Heat olive oil in a skillet over medium-high heat.
4. Add pork chops and cook for about 7-8 minutes per side, or until fully cooked and internal temperature reaches 145°F (63°C).
5. Remove from heat and let rest for 5 minutes.
6. Garnish with chopped parsley and serve with lemon wedges on the side.

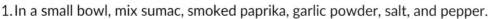

CHICKEN SOUVLAKI WITH TZATZIKI

 15 Mins 10 Mins Serves: 2

- 2 chicken breasts, cut into cubes
- 2 tablespoons olive oil
- 1 tablespoon lemon juice
- 2 cloves garlic, minced
- 1 teaspoon dried oregano
- Salt and pepper, to taste
- 1 cup Greek yogurt
- 1 small cucumber, grated and drained
- 1 tablespoon fresh dill, chopped
- 1 tablespoon olive oil
- Salt and pepper, to taste
- Lemon wedges and pita bread, for serving

360	Calories
36g	Protein
9g	Carbs
20g	Fat

1. In a bowl, combine olive oil, lemon juice, minced garlic, oregano, salt, and pepper. Add chicken cubes and let marinate for at least 30 minutes.
2. In another bowl, mix Greek yogurt with grated cucumber, dill, olive oil, and season with salt and pepper. Chill until ready to serve. Skewer the marinated chicken.
3. Heat a grill or grill pan to medium-high. Grill the skewers, turning occasionally, until chicken is thoroughly cooked, about 10 minutes.
4. Accompany the chicken souvlaki with tzatziki sauce, lemon wedges, and warm pita bread.

GARLIC BUTTER LAMB STEAKS

 10 Mins    15 Mins   Serves: 2

INGREDIENTS

- 2 lamb steaks (about 6 ounces each)
- 2 tablespoons butter
- 2 cloves garlic, minced
- 1 teaspoon fresh rosemary, chopped
- 1 teaspoon fresh thyme, chopped
- Salt and pepper to taste
- 1 tablespoon olive oil

Calories 350
Protein 25g
Carbs 1g
Fat 28g

1. Heat olive oil in a skillet over medium-high heat.
2. Sprinkle lamb steaks with salt and pepper on both sides.
3. Place lamb in the hot skillet. Cook for about 4-5 minutes per side for medium-rare, or until desired doneness.
4. In the last minute of cooking, add butter, garlic, rosemary, and thyme to the skillet. As the butter melts, spoon it continuously over the steaks.
5. Remove lamb from the skillet and let rest for a few minutes before serving. Drizzle the garlic herb butter from the pan over the steaks when serving.

PORK LOIN WITH MEDITERRANEAN HERBS

 10 Mins    20 Mins   Serves: 2

INGREDIENTS

- 1 pound pork loin
- 2 tablespoons olive oil
- 1 teaspoon dried rosemary
- 1 teaspoon dried thyme
- 1 teaspoon dried oregano
- 2 cloves garlic, minced
- Salt and pepper to taste
- 1/2 lemon, juiced

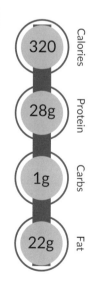

Calories 320
Protein 28g
Carbs 1g
Fat 22g

DIRECTIONS:

1. Rub pork loin with olive oil, garlic, herbs, salt, and pepper. Let marinate for 10 minutes.
2. Preheat your oven to 375°F (190°C).
3. Roast for 20 minutes or until internal temperature reaches 145°F (63°C).
4. Rest for 5 minutes under foil.
5. Slice, drizzle with lemon juice, and serve.

SIMPLE BEEF GYROS

| 🕐 10 Mins | ⏳ 10 Mins | 👥 Serves: 2 |

INGREDIENTS

- 1/2 pound beef strips
- 1 tablespoon olive oil
- 1 teaspoon dried oregano
- 1 garlic clove, minced
- Salt and pepper to taste
- 2 pita breads
- 1/4 cup Greek yogurt
- 1/4 cucumber, diced
- 1/2 tomato, diced
- 1/4 red onion, thinly sliced
- Fresh parsley for garnish

397 Calories
23g Protein
20g Carbs
25g Fat

DIRECTIONS:

1. Season beef strips with olive oil, oregano, garlic, salt, and pepper.
2. Cook beef in a skillet over medium heat for 5-7 minutes until browned.
3. Warm pita breads on a skillet or in the oven.
4. Spread Greek yogurt on each pita, add beef, cucumber, tomato, and red onion.
5. Garnish with fresh parsley and serve immediately.

LAMB MEATBALLS WITH CUCUMBER YOGURT SAUCE

| 🕐 15 Mins | ⏳ 30 Mins | 👥 Serves: 2 |

INGREDIENTS

- 1/2 pound ground beef
- 1/4 cup breadcrumbs
- 1 egg
- 1 garlic clove, minced
- 1/2 teaspoon smoked paprika
- 1/4 teaspoon cumin
- 1 cup canned tomatoes, crushed
- 1/4 cup sherry
- 1 onion, finely chopped
- 2 tablespoons olive oil
- Salt and pepper to taste
- Fresh parsley, chopped for garnish

450 Calories
30g Protein
15g Carbs
30g Fat

DIRECTIONS:

1. Combine beef, breadcrumbs, egg, spices, and season. Form into meatballs.
2. Brown in skillet with olive oil, remove.
3. Cook onion in same skillet, add sherry, reduce. Add tomatoes, simmer.
4. Return meatballs to skillet, cover, simmer 20 minutes. Garnish with parsley.

TOMATO BASIL CHICKEN

⏰ 10 Mins ⏳ 20 Mins 👥 Serves: 2

INGREDIENTS

- 2 boneless, skinless chicken breasts
- 1 tablespoon olive oil
- 2 cloves garlic, minced
- 1 cup cherry tomatoes, halved
- 1/4 cup fresh basil leaves, chopped
- 1/4 cup balsamic vinegar
- Salt and pepper to taste

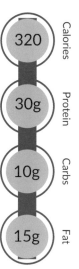

320 Calories
30g Protein
10g Carbs
15g Fat

1. Season the chicken breasts with salt and pepper. In a skillet, heat olive oil over medium heat. Add chicken and cook for 6-8 minutes per side until golden and cooked through.
2. Add minced garlic and halved cherry tomatoes to the skillet. Cook for 2-3 minutes until tomatoes soften.
3. Pour balsamic vinegar over the chicken and tomatoes, stirring to coat the chicken. Simmer for 2 minutes.
4. Remove from heat and sprinkle with fresh basil. Serve hot.

MEDITERRANEAN TURKEY BURGERS

⏰ 10 Mins ⏳ 15 Mins 👥 Serves: 2

- 1/2 pound ground turkey
- 1/4 cup crumbled feta cheese
- 1/4 cup chopped spinach (fresh or thawed frozen)
- 1 garlic clove, minced
- 1 teaspoon dried oregano
- 1 tablespoon olive oil
- Salt and pepper to taste
- 2 whole wheat burger buns
- Optional toppings: sliced cucumber, tomato, red onion, and tzatziki sauce

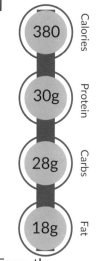

380 Calories
30g Protein
28g Carbs
18g Fat

1. In a bowl, combine ground turkey, feta cheese, spinach, garlic, oregano, salt, and pepper. Form the mixture into two burger patties.
2. Heat olive oil in a skillet over medium heat. Cook the turkey patties for 6-7 minutes per side or until fully cooked through.
3. Toast the burger buns if desired. Place the cooked turkey patties on the buns and top with cucumber, tomato, red onion, and tzatziki sauce if using.
4. Enjoy your Mediterranean turkey burgers warm.

BALSAMIC GLAZED BEEF STEAKS

 10 Mins ⧗ 15 Mins 👥 Serves: 2

INGREDIENTS

- 2 beef steaks (about 6 oz each)
- 2 tablespoons balsamic vinegar
- 1 tablespoon olive oil
- 1 tablespoon honey
- 1 garlic clove, minced
- Salt and pepper to taste
- Fresh thyme or rosemary for garnish (optional)

380 Calories
30g Protein
10g Carbs
22g Fat

DIRECTIONS:

1. Whisk balsamic vinegar, honey, olive oil, garlic, salt, and pepper.
2. Coat steaks with marinade and let sit for 10 minutes.
3. Preheat skillet or grill on medium-high. Cook steaks 4-5 minutes per side for medium-rare.
4. Pour remaining marinade over steaks in the last minute, allowing it to thicken.
5. Let steaks rest, garnish with herbs, and serve hot.

ROSEMARY LAMB SKEWERS

 10 Mins ⧗ 10 Mins 👥 Serves: 2

INGREDIENTS

- 1/2 pound lamb, cubed
- 2 tablespoons olive oil
- 1 tablespoon fresh rosemary, chopped
- 2 cloves garlic, minced
- Salt and pepper, to taste
- Lemon wedges, for serving

320 Calories
25g Protein
3g Carbs
23g Fat

DIRECTIONS:

1. In a bowl, combine olive oil, rosemary, garlic, salt, and pepper.
2. Add lamb cubes to the mixture, toss to coat, and marinate for at least 10 minutes.
3. Thread lamb onto skewers.
4. Preheat grill to medium-high heat and grill skewers for 8-10 minutes, turning occasionally until cooked through.
5. Serve hot with lemon wedges.

From The Sea

PAN-SEARED COD WITH LEMON BUTTER SAUCE

⏱ 5 Mins ⏳ 10 Mins 👥 Serves: 2

INGREDIENTS

- 2 cod fillets (6 ounces each)
- 2 tablespoons unsalted butter
- 1 lemon, juiced and zested
- 1 tablespoon olive oil
- Salt and pepper to taste
- Fresh parsley, chopped (for garnish)

280 Calories
27g Protein
1g Carbs
18g Fat

DIRECTIONS:

1. Sprinkle cod with salt and pepper.
2. In a hot skillet with olive oil, cook cod for about 3-4 minutes per side until golden.
3. Lower heat, add butter, lemon juice, and zest to the skillet, stirring until butter melts.
4. Drizzle sauce over cod, garnish with parsley, and serve immediately.

MUSSELS IN WHITE WINE AND GARLIC SAUCE

⏱ 10 Mins ⏳ 10 Mins 👥 Serves: 2

- 2 pounds fresh mussels, cleaned and debearded
- 1/2 cup dry white wine (use a low-sodium alternative if needed)
- 3 cloves garlic, minced
- 2 tablespoons unsalted butter
- 1 small onion, finely chopped
- 1 tablespoon parsley, chopped
- 1 lemon, juiced
- 1 tablespoon olive oil
- Salt and pepper to taste

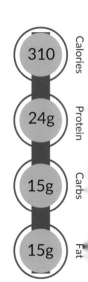
310 Calories
24g Protein
15g Carbs
15g Fat

1. Heat olive oil in a large pot over medium heat. Add garlic and onion, sauté until translucent.
2. Add mussels to the pot, pour in white wine, and sprinkle with salt and pepper. Cover and steam until mussels open, about 5-7 minutes.
3. Once mussels open, reduce heat, add butter, and stir until melted. Finish with lemon juice.
4. Discard any mussels that do not open. Sprinkle with parsley and serve hot with crusty bread if desired.

MUSSELS WITH TOMATO AND BASIL BROTH

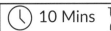 10 Mins 10 Mins Serves: 2

INGREDIENTS

- 2 pounds mussels, cleaned and debearded
- 1 cup canned diced tomatoes
- 1/4 cup fresh basil leaves, chopped
- 2 cloves garlic, minced
- 1/2 cup white wine (or low-sodium vegetable broth)
- 2 tablespoons olive oil
- Salt and pepper to taste
- Lemon wedges for serving

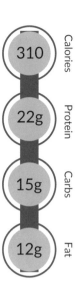

310 Calories
22g Protein
15g Carbs
12g Fat

DIRECTIONS:

1. In a large pot, heat olive oil over medium heat. Add garlic and cook until fragrant, about 1 minute.
2. Stir in diced tomatoes and white wine. Bring to a simmer.
3. Add mussels to the pot, cover, and cook until all mussels have opened, about 5-7 minutes. Discard any that do not open.
4. Stir in chopped basil, and season with salt and pepper.
5. Serve the mussels in their broth with lemon wedges on the side.

GARLIC AND HERB POACHED SALMON

5 Mins 15 Mins Serves: 2

INGREDIENTS

- 2 salmon fillets (about 6 oz each)
- 2 cups low-sodium vegetable or chicken broth
- 2 cloves garlic, minced
- 1 tablespoon fresh parsley, chopped
- 1 tablespoon fresh dill, chopped
- 1 tablespoon olive oil
- 1 lemon, sliced
- Salt and pepper, to taste

280 Calories
30g Protein
2g Carbs
17g Fat

1. In a large skillet, heat broth, garlic, and olive oil over medium heat.
2. Once simmering, add salmon fillets, lemon slices, parsley, and dill.
3. Cover and poach salmon for 10-12 minutes until the fish is cooked through and flakes easily with a fork.
4. Remove the salmon from the skillet and let rest for 2 minutes.
5. Serve hot, garnished with extra fresh herbs and lemon slices.

SHRIMP FETTUCCINE WITH SUN-DRIED TOMATO PESTO

⏱ 10 Mins   ⧖ 15 Mins   👥 Serves: 2

INGREDIENTS

- 6 oz fettuccine
- 1/2 lb shrimp, peeled and deveined
- 1/4 cup sun-dried tomatoes, chopped
- 1/4 cup grated Parmesan cheese
- 2 tbsp olive oil
- 2 cloves garlic, minced
- 1 tbsp fresh basil, chopped
- Salt and pepper to taste
- 1/2 tsp red pepper flakes (optional)

480 Calories
32g Protein
54g Carbs
16g Fat

DIRECTIONS:

1. Cook fettuccine according to package instructions. Drain and set aside.
2. In a pan, heat olive oil over medium heat. Add garlic and sauté until fragrant.
3. Add shrimp, cooking until pink and fully cooked, about 3-4 minutes.
4. Stir in sun-dried tomatoes, Parmesan, and basil. Toss cooked fettuccine into the pan, mixing well to coat.
5. Season with salt, pepper, and red pepper flakes (if using). Serve hot.

SEAFOOD RISOTTO WITH ASPARAGUS

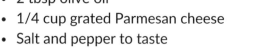

⏱ 10 Mins   ⧖ 20 Mins   👥 Serves: 2

- 1/2 cup Arborio rice
- 1/2 lb mixed seafood (shrimp, scallops, and calamari)
- 1 cup asparagus, trimmed and cut into 1-inch pieces
- 2 cups low-sodium vegetable broth
- 1/4 cup white wine (optional)
- 1 small onion, finely chopped
- 2 cloves garlic, minced
- 2 tbsp olive oil
- 1/4 cup grated Parmesan cheese
- Salt and pepper to taste

460 Calories
30g Protein
52g Carbs
12g Fat

1. Heat olive oil in a pan, sauté onion and garlic until soft.
2. Add Arborio rice, cook for 1-2 minutes.
3. Pour in white wine (optional), then gradually add broth, stirring until rice is tender, about 15 minutes.
4. Add seafood and asparagus, cook 5 more minutes until both are done.
5. Stir in Parmesan, season with salt and pepper, garnish with parsley. Serve hot.

MEDITERRANEAN GRILLED OCTOPUS WITH OLIVE TAPENADE

| ⏰ 10 Mins | ⏳ 15 Mins | 👥 Serves: 2 |

INGREDIENTS

- 1 small octopus (about 1 lb), cleaned
- 2 tablespoons olive oil
- 1 tablespoon lemon juice
- 1 clove garlic, minced
- Salt and pepper to taste
- 1/4 cup black olive tapenade
- Fresh parsley for garnish
- Lemon wedges for serving

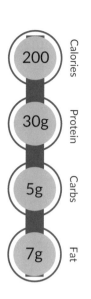

Calories 200
Protein 30g
Carbs 5g
Fat 7g

DIRECTIONS:

1. In a bowl, coat the octopus with olive oil, lemon juice, minced garlic, salt, and pepper.
2. Preheat grill to medium-high heat. Grill the octopus for 3-4 minutes per side, until slightly charred and tender.
3. Once cooked, slice the octopus tentacles.
4. Serve the grilled octopus with olive tapenade on the side. Garnish with fresh parsley and lemon wedges.

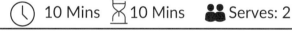

GARLIC SHRIMP WITH SUN-DRIED TOMATOES

| ⏰ 10 Mins | ⏳ 10 Mins | 👥 Serves: 2 |

INGREDIENTS

- 1/2 pound shrimp, peeled and deveined
- 2 tablespoons olive oil
- 3 cloves garlic, minced
- 1/4 cup sun-dried tomatoes, chopped
- 1/4 teaspoon red pepper flakes (optional)
- 1 tablespoon lemon juice
- Salt and pepper to taste
- Fresh parsley, chopped for garnish

Calories 250
Protein 28g
Carbs 6g
Fat 12g

1. Heat olive oil in a skillet over medium heat. Add minced garlic and cook for 1-2 minutes until fragrant.
2. Add the shrimp to the skillet and cook for 2-3 minutes on each side, until pink and opaque.
3. Stir in the sun-dried tomatoes, red pepper flakes (if using), and lemon juice. Cook for another minute to combine the flavors.
4. Season with salt and pepper to taste.
5. Garnish with fresh parsley and serve hot.

BAKED TILAPIA WITH CHERRY TOMATOES AND OLIVES

| ⏱ 5 Mins | ⏳ 15 Mins | 👥 Serves: 2 |

INGREDIENTS

- 2 tilapia fillets
- 1 cup cherry tomatoes, halved
- 1/4 cup pitted Kalamata olives, sliced
- 2 tablespoons olive oil
- 1 tablespoon lemon juice
- 2 cloves garlic, minced
- 1/2 teaspoon dried oregano
- Salt and pepper to taste
- Fresh parsley, chopped for garnish

300 Calories
35g Protein
6g Carbs
15g Fat

DIRECTIONS:

1. Preheat oven to 375°F (190°C).
2. Place the tilapia fillets in a baking dish. Drizzle with olive oil and lemon juice.
3. Scatter cherry tomatoes, olives, and minced garlic over the tilapia. Sprinkle with oregano, salt, and pepper.
4. Bake in the preheated oven for 15 minutes or until the fish is opaque and flakes easily with a fork.
5. Garnish with fresh parsley and serve hot.

COD WITH TOMATO AND CAPERS

| ⏱ 5 Mins | ⏳ 15 Mins | 👥 Serves: 2 |

INGREDIENTS

- 2 cod fillets
- 1 cup diced tomatoes (fresh or canned)
- 2 tablespoons capers, rinsed
- 2 tablespoons olive oil
- 2 cloves garlic, minced
- 1 tablespoon lemon juice
- 1/2 teaspoon dried oregano
- Salt and pepper to taste
- Fresh parsley, chopped for garnish

280 Calories
35g Protein
7g Carbs
12g Fat

1. In a pan, heat olive oil over medium heat. Add minced garlic and sauté for 1-2 minutes until fragrant.
2. Stir in the diced tomatoes and cook for 3-4 minutes until they soften.
3. Add the capers, oregano, and lemon juice. Season with salt and pepper, and let the sauce simmer for 5 minutes.
4. Place the cod fillets in the sauce, cover, and cook for 10 minutes, or until the cod is opaque and flakes easily with a fork. Garnish with fresh parsley and serve hot.

SHRIMP SAGANAKI WITH FETA AND TOMATOES

| (clock) 5 Mins | (hourglass) 15 Mins | (people) Serves: 2 |

INGREDIENTS

- 1/2 pound shrimp, peeled and deveined
- 1 cup diced tomatoes (fresh or canned)
- 2 tablespoons olive oil
- 2 cloves garlic, minced
- 1/4 teaspoon red pepper flakes (optional)
- 1/2 cup crumbled feta cheese
- 1 tablespoon fresh parsley, chopped
- 1 tablespoon lemon juice
- Salt and pepper to taste

350 Calories
28g Protein
9g Carbs
23g Fat

1. Heat olive oil in a skillet, sauté garlic and red pepper flakes for 1-2 minutes. Add diced tomatoes and cook for 4-5 minutes until softened and slightly reduced.
2. Add tomatoes, cook for 4-5 minutes until softened. Add shrimp, cook for 3-4 minutes, turning once until pink.
3. Remove from heat, stir in feta until slightly melted.
4. Drizzle with lemon juice, garnish with parsley, season with salt and pepper. Serve hot.

GRILLED TILAPIA WITH MEDITERRANEAN SALSA VERDE

| (clock) 5 Mins | (hourglass) 15 Mins | (people) Serves: 2 |

- 2 tilapia fillets
- 2 tablespoons olive oil
- 1 garlic clove, minced
- Juice of 1 lemon
- Salt and pepper to taste

For Salsa Verde:
- 1/4 cup fresh parsley, chopped
- 2 tablespoons capers, rinsed
- 2 tablespoons green olives, chopped
- 1 tablespoon lemon juice
- 1 tablespoon olive oil
- 1 teaspoon red wine vinegar

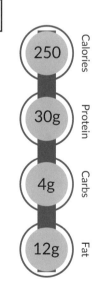

250 Calories
30g Protein
4g Carbs
12g Fat

1. In a small bowl, combine parsley, capers, olives, lemon juice, olive oil, and vinegar. Stir well and set aside.
2. Rub tilapia fillets with olive oil, garlic, lemon juice, salt, and pepper.
3. Preheat grill to medium-high heat. Grill tilapia fillets for 4-6 minutes per side, or until fish is opaque and flakes easily with a fork.
4. Plate the grilled tilapia and spoon the Mediterranean Salsa Verde over the top. Serve immediately.

HERBED GRILLED SWORDFISH STEAKS

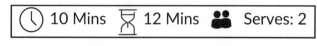
🕐 10 Mins ⧗ 12 Mins 👥 Serves: 2

INGREDIENTS

- 2 swordfish steaks (about 6 oz each)
- 2 tablespoons olive oil
- 1 tablespoon lemon juice
- 1 garlic clove, minced
- 1 teaspoon fresh rosemary, chopped
- 1 teaspoon fresh thyme, chopped
- Salt and pepper to taste

280 Calories
30g Protein
2g Carbs
18g Fat

DIRECTIONS:

1. In a small bowl, whisk together olive oil, lemon juice, garlic, rosemary, thyme, salt, and pepper. Coat swordfish steaks with the marinade and let sit for 10 minutes.
2. Preheat grill to medium-high heat.
3. Place swordfish steaks on the grill and cook for 5-6 minutes per side, or until the fish is opaque and flakes easily with a fork.
4. Remove from the grill, drizzle with extra lemon juice if desired, and serve immediately.

CITRUS-INFUSED GRILLED SHRIMP

🕐 10 Mins ⧗ 8 Mins 👥 Serves: 2

INGREDIENTS

- 12 large shrimp, peeled and deveined
- 2 tablespoons olive oil
- 1 tablespoon orange juice
- 1 tablespoon lemon juice
- 1 teaspoon orange zest
- 1 garlic clove, minced
- Salt and pepper to taste
- Fresh parsley for garnish

210 Calories
24g Protein
3g Carbs
12g Fat

DIRECTIONS:

1. In a bowl, mix olive oil, orange juice, lemon juice, orange zest, garlic, salt, and pepper. Add shrimp and let marinate for 10 minutes.
2. Preheat grill or grill pan over medium-high heat.
3. Thread shrimp onto skewers and grill for 3-4 minutes per side, until pink and opaque.
4. Remove from grill, garnish with fresh parsley, and serve immediately.

SPICED OCTOPUS WITH ROASTED VEGETABLES

| 🕐 10 Mins | ⏳ 30 Mins | 👥 Serves: 2 |

INGREDIENTS

- 1 pound octopus, cleaned
- 1 tablespoon olive oil
- 1 teaspoon smoked paprika
- 1/2 teaspoon cumin
- 1 garlic clove, minced
- Salt and pepper to taste
- 1 zucchini, sliced
- 1 red bell pepper, chopped
- 1 small red onion, sliced
- Fresh parsley for garnish

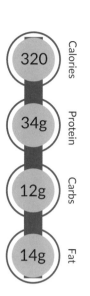

320	Calories
34g	Protein
12g	Carbs
14g	Fat

DIRECTIONS:

1. Preheat oven to 400°F (200°C).
2. Toss zucchini, red bell pepper, and onion with olive oil, salt, and pepper. Roast for 20-25 minutes.
3. Mix olive oil, smoked paprika, cumin, garlic, salt, and pepper. Rub over octopus.
4. Grill for 4-5 minutes per side until tender and slightly charred.
5. Plate with roasted vegetables, garnish with parsley, and serve hot.

MEDITERRANEAN STUFFED CALAMARI

| 🕐 15 Mins | ⏳ 20 Mins | 👥 Serves: 2 |

INGREDIENTS

- 6 medium calamari tubes, cleaned
- 1/4 cup cooked quinoa
- 2 tablespoons diced tomatoes
- 2 tablespoons chopped spinach
- 1 tablespoon feta cheese, crumbled
- 1 tablespoon olive oil
- 1 garlic clove, minced
- 1 tablespoon fresh parsley, chopped
- Salt and pepper to taste
- Lemon wedges for serving

210	Calories
22g	Protein
10g	Carbs
9g	Fat

DIRECTIONS:

1. In a bowl, mix quinoa, tomatoes, spinach, feta, garlic, parsley, salt, and pepper.
2. Gently stuff the calamari tubes with the filling, securing the open ends with toothpicks.
3. Heat olive oil in a skillet over medium heat. Sear stuffed calamari for 4-5 minutes on each side until golden brown and cooked through.
4. Garnish with parsley and lemon wedges. Serve immediately.

CLAMS IN GARLIC AND WINE BROTH

 10 Mins | 10 Mins | Serves: 2

INGREDIENTS

- 1 lb fresh clams, cleaned
- 2 tablespoons olive oil
- 3 garlic cloves, minced
- 1/2 cup white wine
- 1/2 cup low-sodium vegetable broth
- 1 tablespoon fresh parsley, chopped
- Salt and pepper to taste
- Lemon wedges for garnish

250 Calories
20g Protein
8g Carbs
10g Fat

DIRECTIONS:

1. Heat olive oil in a large skillet over medium heat. Add minced garlic and sauté for 1-2 minutes until fragrant.
2. Pour in the white wine and vegetable broth, bringing to a simmer.
3. Add the clams, cover, and cook for 5-7 minutes until the clams open.
4. Discard any unopened clams. Stir in chopped parsley and season with salt and pepper.
5. Serve hot with lemon wedges on the side.

GRILLED TILAPIA WITH GARLIC HERB MARINADE

10 Mins | 8 Mins | Serves: 2

INGREDIENTS

- 2 tilapia fillets
- 2 tablespoons olive oil
- 2 garlic cloves, minced
- 1 tablespoon lemon juice
- 1 teaspoon fresh parsley, chopped
- 1 teaspoon fresh thyme, chopped
- Salt and pepper to taste

220 Calories
25g Protein
2g Carbs
12g Fat

1. In a small bowl, mix olive oil, minced garlic, lemon juice, parsley, thyme, salt, and pepper to create the marinade.
2. Coat the tilapia fillets with the marinade and let them sit for at least 10 minutes.
3. Preheat grill or grill pan to medium-high heat.
4. Grill the tilapia for 3-4 minutes per side, until the fish is cooked through and flakes easily with a fork.
5. Serve immediately, garnished with additional fresh herbs if desired.

TILAPIA PICCATA WITH CAPERS AND LEMON

⏱ 10 Mins ⏳ 10 Mins 👥 Serves: 2

INGREDIENTS

- 2 tilapia fillets
- 2 tablespoons olive oil
- 2 tablespoons butter
- 1/4 cup fresh lemon juice
- 1/4 cup chicken broth
- 2 tablespoons capers, drained
- 1 garlic clove, minced
- Salt and pepper to taste
- Fresh parsley, chopped (optional)

320 Calories
25g Protein
3g Carbs
20g Fat

1. Season the tilapia fillets with salt and pepper on both sides.
2. Heat olive oil in a skillet over medium heat. Add the tilapia and cook for 3-4 minutes per side until golden and cooked through. Remove from skillet and set aside.
3. In the same skillet, add butter and garlic, sautéing until fragrant.
4. Add lemon juice, chicken broth, and capers to the skillet. Simmer for 2-3 minutes until the sauce slightly reduces.
5. Return the tilapia to the skillet and spoon the sauce over the fish to coat.
6. Garnish with fresh parsley and serve immediately.

ZESTY LEMON AND DILL TILAPIA FILLETS

⏱ 5 Mins ⏳ 10 Mins 👥 Serves: 2

INGREDIENTS

- 2 tilapia fillets
- 2 tablespoons olive oil
- 2 tablespoons fresh lemon juice
- 1 tablespoon fresh dill, chopped
- 1 garlic clove, minced
- Salt and pepper to taste
- Lemon wedges for garnish

230 Calories
28g Protein
1g Carbs
12g Fat

1. Season the tilapia fillets with salt and pepper.
2. Heat olive oil in a skillet over medium heat. Add the garlic and sauté for 1 minute.
3. Place the tilapia fillets in the skillet and cook for 3-4 minutes per side, until the fish is golden and flakes easily.
4. Remove from heat and drizzle with fresh lemon juice.
5. Sprinkle with fresh dill and garnish with lemon wedges. Serve immediately.

MUSSELS IN A SAFFRON AND GARLIC CREAM SAUCE

🕐 10 Mins ⏳ 15 Mins 👥 Serves: 2

INGREDIENTS

- 1 pound fresh mussels, cleaned
- 1 tablespoon olive oil
- 2 garlic cloves, minced
- 1/4 cup dry white wine
- 1/4 cup heavy cream
- A pinch of saffron threads
- 1/4 teaspoon salt
- Fresh parsley, chopped for garnish
- Lemon wedges for serving

350 Calories
30g Protein
12g Carbs
22g Fat

DIRECTIONS:

1. Heat olive oil in a large pan over medium heat. Add garlic and sauté until fragrant, about 1-2 minutes.
2. Add white wine and saffron, simmer for 2-3 minutes to reduce slightly.
3. Stir in the heavy cream, season with salt and pepper, and bring to a simmer.
4. Add the mussels, cover, and cook for 5-7 minutes until all the mussels have opened.
5. Remove from heat, sprinkle with fresh parsley, and serve with lemon wedges.

MUSSELS WITH CAPERS AND SUN-DRIED TOMATOES

🕐 10 Mins ⏳ 15 Mins 👥 Serves: 2

INGREDIENTS

- 1 lb fresh mussels, cleaned and debearded
- 2 tablespoons olive oil
- 2 garlic cloves, minced
- 1/4 cup sun-dried tomatoes, chopped
- 1 tablespoon capers, drained
- 1/2 cup white wine
- 1/4 cup fresh parsley, chopped
- Salt and pepper to taste
- Lemon wedges for serving

320 Calories
28g Protein
10g Carbs
18g Fat

1. Heat olive oil in a large pan over medium heat. Add garlic and sauté until fragrant, about 1-2 minutes.
2. Stir in sun-dried tomatoes and capers, cooking for 2 minutes.
3. Add white wine and bring to a simmer.
4. Add mussels, cover, and cook for 5-7 minutes, or until all the mussels have opened.
5. Remove from heat, garnish with fresh parsley, and serve with lemon wedges.

CHILLED MUSSELS WITH LEMON CAPER VINAIGRETTE

( ) 10 Mins   ⏳ 15 Mins   👥 Serves: 2

INGREDIENTS

- 1 lb fresh mussels, cleaned and debearded
- 1/4 cup olive oil
- 2 tablespoons lemon juice
- 1 tablespoon capers, drained and chopped
- 1 garlic clove, minced
- 1/4 teaspoon Dijon mustard
- Fresh parsley, chopped for garnish
- Salt and pepper to taste
- Lemon wedges for serving

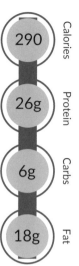

290 Calories
26g Protein
6g Carbs
18g Fat

1. In a large pot, steam mussels in 1 cup of water over medium heat until they open, about 5-7 minutes. Remove from heat and let them cool.
2. In a bowl, whisk together olive oil, lemon juice, capers, garlic, and Dijon mustard. Season with salt and pepper.
3. Remove mussels from their shells and place in a bowl. Toss with the lemon caper vinaigrette.
4. Chill in the fridge for at least 30 minutes before serving.
5. Garnish with fresh parsley and serve with lemon wedges.

GRILLED SALMON WITH OLIVE AND CAPER RELISH

( ) 10 Mins   ⏳ 10 Mins   👥 Serves: 2

INGREDIENTS

- 2 salmon fillets (about 6 oz each)
- 2 tablespoons olive oil
- Salt and pepper to taste
- 1/4 cup green olives, chopped
- 1 tablespoon capers, rinsed and chopped
- 1 tablespoon lemon juice
- 1 garlic clove, minced
- Fresh parsley, chopped for garnish

350 Calories
23g Protein
4g Carbs
22g Fat

1. Preheat grill to medium-high heat. Drizzle salmon fillets with 1 tablespoon of olive oil and season with salt and pepper.
2. Grill salmon for 4-5 minutes per side, until cooked through and lightly charred.
3. While the salmon is grilling, mix together the chopped olives, capers, lemon juice, garlic, and remaining olive oil in a bowl to make the relish.
4. Once the salmon is done, remove from the grill and top with the olive and caper relish.
5. Garnish with fresh parsley and serve immediately.

BALSAMIC GLAZED SALMON WITH ROSEMARY

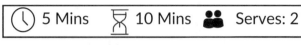
⏱ 5 Mins ⏳ 10 Mins 👥 Serves: 2

INGREDIENTS
- 2 salmon fillets (about 6 oz each)
- 2 tablespoons balsamic vinegar
- 1 tablespoon honey
- 1 tablespoon olive oil
- 1 teaspoon fresh rosemary, chopped
- 1 garlic clove, minced
- Salt and pepper to taste

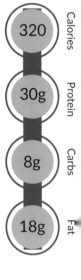
Calories 320 | Protein 30g | Carbs 8g | Fat 18g

1. Preheat a skillet over medium heat and drizzle with olive oil.
2. In a small bowl, whisk together balsamic vinegar, honey, rosemary, and garlic.
3. Season the salmon fillets with salt and pepper and add them to the skillet, skin-side down. Cook for 4-5 minutes, then flip.
4. Pour the balsamic glaze over the salmon and cook for an additional 4-5 minutes, basting with the glaze until the salmon is cooked through and glazed.
5. Remove from heat, let rest for 2 minutes, and serve with extra glaze drizzled over the top.

SALMON WITH SPINACH AND FETA STUFFING

⏱ 10 Mins ⏳ 15 Mins 👥 Serves: 2

INGREDIENTS
- 2 salmon fillets (6 oz each)
- 1 cup fresh spinach, chopped
- 1/4 cup feta cheese, crumbled
- 1 garlic clove, minced
- 1 tablespoon olive oil
- 1 teaspoon lemon juice
- Salt and pepper to taste

Calories 380 | Protein 35g | Carbs 5g | Fat 23g

1. Preheat oven to 375°F (190°C).
2. In a skillet, heat olive oil over medium heat. Sauté garlic until fragrant, then add spinach and cook until wilted. Stir in feta cheese and lemon juice.
3. Cut a pocket into each salmon fillet. Stuff each pocket with the spinach and feta mixture.
4. Season the salmon with salt and pepper and place on a baking sheet.
5. Bake in the preheated oven for 12-15 minutes, until the salmon is cooked through.
6. Serve hot, garnished with a lemon wedge if desired.

SPICY SHRIMP WITH MEDITERRANEAN QUINOA

(○) 10 Mins   ⏳ 20 Mins   👥 Serves: 2

- 1/2 cup quinoa, rinsed
- 1 cup water or low-sodium vegetable broth
- 1/2 pound shrimp, peeled and deveined
- 1 tablespoon olive oil
- 1 clove garlic, minced
- 1 teaspoon paprika
- 1/4 teaspoon cayenne pepper
- 1/4 teaspoon ground cumin
- 1/2 cup cherry tomatoes, halved
- 1/4 cup Kalamata olives, sliced
- 1 tablespoon lemon juice
- Fresh parsley, chopped for garnish
- Salt and pepper to taste

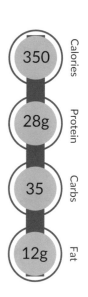

350 Calories
28g Protein
35 Carbs
12g Fat

DIRECTIONS:

1. Bring quinoa and water (or broth) to a boil. Cover and simmer for 15 minutes until fluffy.
2. Toss shrimp with olive oil, garlic, paprika, cayenne, cumin, salt, and pepper.
3. Cook shrimp in a skillet over medium heat for 3-4 minutes per side until pink.
4. Mix quinoa with cherry tomatoes, olives, and lemon juice. Adjust seasoning.
5. Plate quinoa, top with shrimp, and garnish with parsley. Serve immediately.

COD IN A WHITE WINE AND CAPER SAUCE

(○) 10 Mins   ⏳ 15Mins   👥 Serves: 2

INGREDIENTS

- 2 cod fillets
- 1 tablespoon olive oil
- 2 cloves garlic, minced
- 1/4 cup white wine
- 1 tablespoon capers, rinsed
- 1 tablespoon lemon juice
- 1/4 cup vegetable or chicken broth
- Salt and pepper to taste
- Fresh parsley for garnish

250 Calories
30g Protein
4g Carbs
10g Fat

1. Heat olive oil in a skillet over medium heat. Add garlic and sauté for 1-2 minutes until fragrant.
2. Add cod fillets to the skillet and cook for 3-4 minutes per side, until opaque and flaky. Remove and set aside.
3. In the same skillet, add white wine, capers, lemon juice, and broth. Simmer for 5 minutes until slightly reduced.
4. Return cod to the skillet and spoon the sauce over the fillets. Cook for 1-2 more minutes.

COD FILLETS WITH OLIVE AND FETA CRUST

⏱ 10 Mins ⧗ 15 Mins 👥 Serves: 2

INGREDIENTS

- 2 cod fillets
- 1/4 cup black olives, pitted and chopped
- 2 tablespoons crumbled feta cheese
- 1 tablespoon olive oil
- 1 tablespoon lemon juice
- 1 teaspoon dried oregano
- Salt and pepper to taste

280 Calories
32g Protein
3g Carbs
15g Fat

1. Preheat oven to 375°F (190°C).
2. In a small bowl, mix chopped olives, feta cheese, olive oil, lemon juice, oregano, salt, and pepper.
3. Place cod fillets on a baking sheet lined with parchment paper.
4. Spoon the olive and feta mixture over the top of the cod fillets, pressing gently to adhere.
5. Bake in the preheated oven for 12-15 minutes until the cod is opaque and flakes easily with a fork.
6. Serve hot, garnished with extra lemon wedges if desired.

BAKED COD WITH BASIL AND TOMATO RELISH

⏱ 10 Mins ⧗ 15 Mins 👥 Serves: 2

INGREDIENTS

- 2 cod fillets
- 1 cup cherry tomatoes, halved
- 1/4 cup fresh basil, chopped
- 1 tablespoon olive oil
- 1 tablespoon lemon juice
- 1 garlic clove, minced
- Salt and pepper to taste

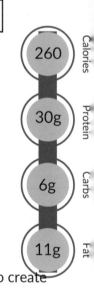

260 Calories
30g Protein
6g Carbs
11g Fat

1. Preheat oven to 375°F (190°C).
2. In a bowl, combine cherry tomatoes, basil, olive oil, lemon juice, garlic, salt, and pepper to create the relish.
3. Place cod fillets on a baking sheet lined with parchment paper.
4. Spoon the basil and tomato relish over the cod fillets, covering them evenly.
5. Bake in the preheated oven for 12-15 minutes until the cod is opaque and flakes easily with a fork.
6. Serve hot with an extra drizzle of lemon juice, if desired.

After Dinner
and in Between

HONEY AND THYME ROASTED PEARS

🕐 5 Mins   ⏳ 20 Mins   👥 Serves: 2

INGREDIENTS

- 2 ripe pears, halved and cored
- 2 tablespoons honey
- 1 tablespoon olive oil
- 1/2 teaspoon fresh thyme leaves
- 1/4 teaspoon ground cinnamon
- 1 tablespoon lemon juice

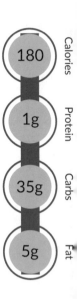
180 Calories
1g Protein
35g Carbs
5g Fat

DIRECTIONS:

1. Preheat oven to 375°F (190°C).
2. Place pear halves in a baking dish, cut side up.
3. Drizzle with honey, olive oil, and lemon juice. Sprinkle with thyme leaves and cinnamon.
4. Roast for 20 minutes, or until pears are tender and caramelized.
5. Serve warm with an extra drizzle of honey, if desired.

LEMON AND OLIVE OIL CAKE

🕐 10 Mins   ⏳ 25 Mins   👥 Serves: 2

- 1/2 cup all-purpose flour
- 1/4 cup sugar
- 1/4 teaspoon baking powder
- 1/8 teaspoon baking soda
- 1/8 teaspoon salt
- 1 large egg
- 1/4 cup extra virgin olive oil
- Zest of 1 lemon
- 2 tablespoons fresh lemon juice
- 1/4 teaspoon vanilla extract

290 Calories
4g Protein
35g Carbs
15g Fat

1. Preheat oven to 350°F (175°C). Grease a small baking pan or line with parchment paper.
2. In a bowl, whisk together flour, sugar, baking powder, baking soda, and salt.
3. In a separate bowl, mix egg, olive oil, lemon zest, lemon juice, and vanilla extract until smooth.
4. Gradually combine the wet ingredients with the dry ingredients, stirring until a smooth batter forms.
5. Pour the batter into the prepared baking pan and spread evenly.
6. Bake for 25 minutes, or until a toothpick inserted in the center comes out clean.
7. Let cool before slicing and serving.

CANNOLI WITH RICOTTA AND PISTACHIO FILLING

| ⏱ 15 Mins | ⏳ 0 Mins | 👥 Serves: 2 |

INGREDIENTS

- 4 cannoli shells
- 1/2 cup ricotta cheese
- 2 tablespoons powdered sugar
- 1/4 cup chopped pistachios
- 1/2 teaspoon vanilla extract
- 1 tablespoon mini chocolate chips (optional)
- Zest of 1 lemon (optional)

280	Calories
8g	Protein
34g	Carbs
12g	Fat

1. In a bowl, mix ricotta cheese, powdered sugar, vanilla extract, and lemon zest (if using) until smooth.
2. Stir in chopped pistachios and mini chocolate chips (optional).
3. Spoon the mixture into a piping bag or use a spoon to fill each cannoli shell with the ricotta filling.
4. Garnish the ends with extra chopped pistachios.
5. Serve immediately or refrigerate for a firmer filling.

MEDITERRANEAN DATE AND NUT BALLS

| ⏱ 10 Mins | ⏳ 0 Mins | 👥 Serves: 2 |

INGREDIENTS

- 1/2 cup dates, pitted
- 1/4 cup almonds
- 1/4 cup walnuts
- 1 tablespoon honey
- 1 teaspoon cinnamon
- 1 tablespoon sesame seeds

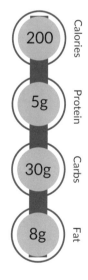

200	Calories
5g	Protein
30g	Carbs
8g	Fat

DIRECTIONS:

1. Blend dates, almonds, walnuts, honey, and cinnamon in a food processor until smooth.
2. Roll the mixture into small balls using your hands.
3. Roll each ball in sesame seeds to coat.
4. Refrigerate for 10 minutes to firm up before serving.

VANILLA PANNA COTTA WITH BERRY COMPOTE

| ⏱ 10 Mins | ⏳ 5 Mins | 👥 Serves: 2 |

For the Panna Cotta:
- 1 cup heavy cream
- 1/4 cup milk
- 1 tablespoon honey
- 1/2 teaspoon vanilla extract
- 1 teaspoon gelatin
- 1 tablespoon cold water

For the Berry Compote:
- 1/2 cup mixed berries (strawberries, raspberries, blueberries)
- 1 tablespoon honey
- 1 teaspoon lemon juice

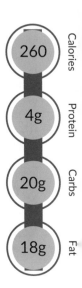

260 Calories
4g Protein
20g Carbs
18g Fat

DIRECTIONS:

1. Sprinkle gelatin over water and let sit 5 minutes.
2. Warm cream, milk, honey, and vanilla until simmering. Stir in gelatin until dissolved.
3. Pour into ramekins and chill for 4 hours.
4. Heat berries, honey, and lemon juice until soft.
5. Top panna cotta with compote and serve chilled.

APRICOT AND WALNUT STUFFED DATES

| ⏱ 5 Mins | ⏳ 0 Mins | 👥 Serves: 2 |

INGREDIENTS

- 6 large Medjool dates, pitted
- 6 dried apricots, chopped
- 6 walnut halves
- 1 tablespoon honey (optional)
- Pinch of cinnamon (optional)

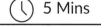

180 Calories
3g Protein
38g Carbs
5g Fat

DIRECTIONS:

1. Slice each date lengthwise and remove the pit.
2. Stuff each date with a few pieces of chopped apricot and a walnut half.
3. Drizzle with honey and sprinkle with a pinch of cinnamon, if desired.
4. Serve immediately or refrigerate for a chilled treat.

PISTACHIO RICE PUDDING

⏰ 5 Mins   ⧗ 25 Mins   👥 Serves: 2

INGREDIENTS

- 1/4 cup short-grain rice
- 1 1/2 cups milk
- 1/4 cup sugar
- 1/4 cup chopped pistachios
- 1/2 teaspoon vanilla extract
- 1/4 teaspoon ground cinnamon (optional)

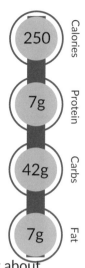

Calories 250
Protein 7g
Carbs 42g
Fat 7g

1. Rinse the rice and add it to a pot with milk. Cook over medium heat, stirring frequently, for about 15 minutes.
2. Stir in sugar and cinnamon (if using), then continue cooking and stirring for another 10 minutes, or until the mixture thickens.
3. Add vanilla extract and remove from heat.
4. Let the pudding cool slightly, then top with chopped pistachios.
5. Serve warm or chilled, as desired.

BAKED APPLES WITH CINNAMON AND ALMONDS

⏰ 10 Mins   ⧗ 25 Mins   👥 Serves: 2

INGREDIENTS

- 2 medium apples, cored
- 2 tablespoons honey
- 1 teaspoon ground cinnamon
- 2 tablespoons chopped almonds
- 1 tablespoon raisins (optional)
- 1 teaspoon lemon juice
- 1/2 teaspoon vanilla extract

DIRECTIONS:

Calories 210
Protein 2g
Carbs 40g
Fat 5g

1. Preheat oven to 350°F (175°C).
2. Core the apples and place them in a baking dish.
3. In a small bowl, mix honey, cinnamon, almonds, raisins (if using), lemon juice, and vanilla extract.
4. Fill the cored apples with the almond mixture.
5. Bake for 25 minutes or until apples are tender.
6. Serve warm.

LEMON RICOTTA CHEESECAKE

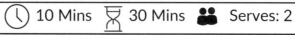
🕐 10 Mins ⏳ 30 Mins 👥 Serves: 2

INGREDIENTS

- 1 cup ricotta cheese
- 2 tablespoons honey
- 1 large egg
- 1 teaspoon lemon zest
- 1 tablespoon fresh lemon juice
- 1/4 teaspoon vanilla extract
- 1 tablespoon flour
- Pinch of salt

210 Calories
9g Protein
18g Carbs
12g Fat

1. Preheat oven to 350°F (175°C). Grease two small ramekins.
2. In a bowl, mix ricotta, honey, egg, lemon zest, lemon juice, and vanilla extract until smooth.
3. Stir in flour and salt until well combined.
4. Pour the mixture into the prepared ramekins.
5. Bake for 25-30 minutes or until the cheesecakes are set and lightly golden on top.
6. Let cool slightly, then serve warm or chilled.

DATE AND WALNUT STUFFED PASTRIES

🕐 10 Mins ⏳ 15 Mins 👥 Serves: 2

INGREDIENTS

- 4 sheets phyllo dough
- 1/2 cup pitted dates, finely chopped
- 1/4 cup walnuts, finely chopped
- 1 tablespoon honey
- 1/2 teaspoon cinnamon
- 2 tablespoons melted butter or olive oil

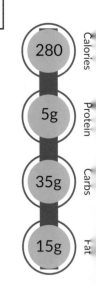
280 Calories
5g Protein
35g Carbs
15g Fat

DIRECTIONS:

1. Preheat oven to 350°F (175°C).
2. Mix dates, walnuts, honey, and cinnamon in a bowl. Layer phyllo dough sheets, brushing each with butter or olive oil.
3. Add date-walnut mixture along one edge, roll, and place on a baking sheet.
4. Brush with more butter or oil.
5. Bake for 12-15 minutes until golden. Serve warm.

SAFFRON AND HONEY PANNA COTTA

INGREDIENTS

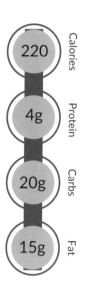

220 Calories
4g Protein
20g Carbs
15g Fat

- 1/2 cup whole milk
- 1/2 cup heavy cream
- 2 tablespoons honey
- 1/2 teaspoon saffron threads
- 1 teaspoon vanilla extract
- 1 1/2 teaspoons unflavored gelatin
- 2 tablespoons cold water

1. In a small bowl, sprinkle the gelatin over the cold water and let it bloom for 5 minutes.
2. In a saucepan, combine milk, cream, honey, and saffron over medium heat. Stir until the mixture is warm, but not boiling.
3. Remove from heat, stir in vanilla extract, and whisk in the bloomed gelatin until fully dissolved.
4. Pour the mixture into serving cups and refrigerate for at least 4 hours, or until set.
5. Serve chilled, optionally drizzling with extra honey.

MEDITERRANEAN SESAME HONEY COOKIES

(10 Mins | 12 Mins | Serves: 2)

INGREDIENTS

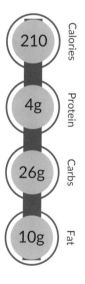

210 Calories
4g Protein
26g Carbs
10g Fat

- 1/2 cup all-purpose flour
- 2 tablespoons honey
- 2 tablespoons olive oil
- 1/4 cup sesame seeds
- 1/4 teaspoon cinnamon
- 1/4 teaspoon baking powder
- Pinch of salt

1. Preheat the oven to 350°F (175°C) and line a baking sheet with parchment paper.
2. In a bowl, mix the flour, baking powder, cinnamon, and salt.
3. Add honey and olive oil to the dry ingredients and mix until a dough forms.
4. Stir in the sesame seeds and combine evenly.
5. Roll the dough into small balls and flatten slightly on the prepared baking sheet.
6. Bake for 10-12 minutes, or until golden brown.
7. Let cool before serving.

FIG AND ALMOND YOGURT PARFAIT

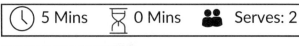

🕐 5 Mins   ⏳ 0 Mins   👥 Serves: 2

INGREDIENTS

- 1 cup Greek yogurt
- 4 fresh figs, quartered
- 2 tablespoons honey
- 1/4 cup almonds, chopped
- 1/4 teaspoon cinnamon
- 2 tablespoons granola (optional)

260 Calories
12g Protein
35g Carbs
10g Fat

DIRECTIONS:

1. Layer half of the Greek yogurt in two glasses or bowls.
2. Drizzle with honey and sprinkle with chopped almonds and cinnamon.
3. Add the fresh figs on top, followed by the remaining yogurt.
4. Top with more almonds and granola if desired.
5. Serve immediately.

CINNAMON-SUGAR LOUKOUMADES (GREEK DONUTS)

🕐 10 Mins   ⏳ 20 Mins   👥 Serves: 2

INGREDIENTS

- 1 cup all-purpose flour
- 1 teaspoon instant yeast
- 1/2 cup warm water
- 1 tablespoon sugar
- 1/4 teaspoon salt
- Vegetable oil (for frying)
- 1/4 cup honey
- 1/4 cup powdered sugar
- 1 teaspoon ground cinnamon

220 Calories
4g Protein
35g Carbs
7g Fat

1. In a bowl, mix flour, yeast, warm water, sugar, and salt to form a smooth batter. Let it sit for 30 minutes to rise.
2. Heat vegetable oil in a deep pan over medium heat.
3. Drop spoonfuls of the dough into the hot oil and fry until golden brown on all sides, about 2-3 minutes per side. Remove and drain on paper towels.
4. Drizzle with honey and toss in a mixture of powdered sugar and cinnamon.
5. Serve warm and enjoy.

PISTACHIO ICE CREAM

⏰ 10 Mins   ⏳ 0 Mins   👥 Serves: 2

INGREDIENTS

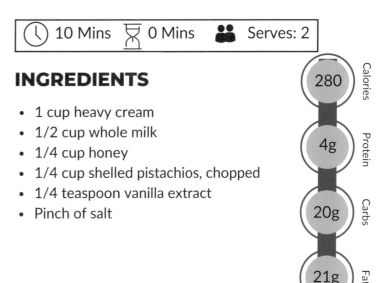

- 1 cup heavy cream
- 1/2 cup whole milk
- 1/4 cup honey
- 1/4 cup shelled pistachios, chopped
- 1/4 teaspoon vanilla extract
- Pinch of salt

280 Calories
4g Protein
20g Carbs
21g Fat

1. In a bowl, whisk together heavy cream, milk, honey, vanilla extract, and salt until smooth.
2. Pour the mixture into an ice cream maker and churn according to the manufacturer's instructions.
3. In the last 5 minutes of churning, add the chopped pistachios.
4. Transfer the churned ice cream to a container and freeze for at least 2 hours or until firm.
5. Serve chilled and garnish with extra pistachios, if desired.

CHOCOLATE TAHINI BROWNIES

⏰ 10 Mins   ⏳ 25 Mins   👥 Serves: 2

INGREDIENTS

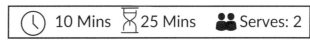

- 1/4 cup tahini
- 1/4 cup dark chocolate chips
- 1/4 cup cocoa powder
- 1/4 cup honey or maple syrup
- 1 egg
- 1/4 teaspoon baking powder
- 1/4 teaspoon vanilla extract
- Pinch of sea salt

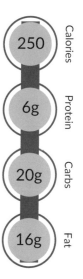

250 Calories
6g Protein
20g Carbs
16g Fat

DIRECTIONS:

1. Preheat oven to 350°F (180°C) and grease a small baking dish.
2. Melt chocolate chips in the microwave.
3. In a bowl, whisk together tahini, honey, egg, vanilla, and melted chocolate.
4. Stir in cocoa powder, baking powder, and salt until smooth.
5. Pour batter into the dish and bake for 20-25 minutes. Cool, slice, and serve.

MEAL PLAN

Breakfast	Lunch	Dinner
Ricotta and Lemon Pancakes	Roast Chicken with Mediterranean Herb Stuffing & Tomato Basil Soup with a Touch of Cream	Seafood Risotto with Asparagus
Avocado and Tomato Toast with Olive Oil Drizzle	Garlic Lemon Chicken Skewers & Roasted Red Pepper and Feta Salad with Fresh Herbs	Garlic Spinach Sauté & Mussels in White Wine and Garlic Sauce
Tomato and Mozzarella Stuffed French Toast	One-Pan Mediterranean Chicken with Olives and Tomatoes & Hearty Chickpea and Spinach Soup	Mediterranean Grilled Vegetable Platter & Pan-Seared Cod with Lemon Butter Sauce
Provencal Vegetable Omelette	Simple Beef Koftas & Lentil and Spinach Salad with Citrus Dressing.	Stuffed Bell Peppers with Quinoa and Feta & Garlic and Herb Poached Salmon
Tomato and Feta Toast with Olive Oil Drizzle	Balsamic Glazed Beef Skewers & Mediterranean Quinoa Salad with Bell Peppers and Olives	Garlic Spinach and Mushroom Sauté & Cod with Tomato and Capers
Olive and Tomato Morning Flatbread	Turkish Meatballs in Tomato Sauce & Grilled Eggplant and Mozzarella Salad	Grilled Zucchini with Lemon and Herbs & Herbed Grilled Swordfish Steaks
Spinach and Feta Breakfast Wraps	Spanish Meatballs with Sherry Tomato Sauce & Greek Lemon Chicken Soup	Herb-Roasted Artichokes & Garlic Shrimp with Sun-Dried Tomatoes
Avocado Egg Scramble Wrap	Pork Tenderloin with Rosemary and Garlic & Simple Greek Salad with Cucumber, Tomato, and Feta	Baked Ratatouille with Crispy Chickpea Topping
Herbed Goat Cheese and Asparagus Frittata.	Mediterranean Turkey Burgers	Seafood Risotto with Asparagus
Almond Butter Toast Delight	Tomato Basil Soup with a Touch of Cream & Rosemary Lamb Skewers	Garlic Spinach Sauté & Baked Cod with Basil and Tomato Relish

Zucchini and Potato Frittata	Herb-Infused Lamb Chops & Beetroot and Orange Salad with Walnuts	Greek Style Green Beans with Tomato and Feta & Tilapia Piccata with Capers and Lemon
Cretan Dakos	Lentil and Spinach Salad with Citrus Dressing & Simple Beef Gyros	Spicy Stuffed Zucchini Boats & Cod Fillets with Olive and Feta Crust
Italian Basil and Tomato Bruschetta	Roasted Red Pepper and Feta Salad with Fresh Herbs & Balsamic Glazed Beef Steaks	Grilled Zucchini with Lemon and Herbs & Salmon with Spinach and Feta Stuffing
Turkish Menemen (Tomato and Egg Scramble)	Hearty Chickpea and Spinach Soup & Pork Loin with Mediterranean Herbs	Mediterranean Grilled Vegetable Platter & Cod in a White Wine and Caper Sauce
Greek Yogurt Parfait with Honey and Walnuts	Mediterranean Quinoa Salad with Bell Peppers and Olives & Garlic Butter Lamb Steaks	Herb-Roasted Artichokes & Balsamic Glazed Salmon with Rosemary
Tomato and Mozzarella Stuffed French Toast	Cauliflower and Tahini Soup & Chicken Souvlaki with Tzatziki	Tomato and Basil Zucchini Noodles & Grilled Tilapia with Garlic Herb Marinade
Avocado and Tomato Toast with Olive Oil Drizzle.	Greek Meatballs with Tzatziki	Seafood Risotto with Asparagus
Mediterranean Morning Smoothie with Greek Yogurt and Berries	Mediterranean Quinoa Salad with Bell Peppers and Olives & Garlic Butter Lamb Steaks	Herb-Roasted Artichokes & Garlic Shrimp with Sun-Dried Tomatoes
Spinach and Feta Breakfast Wraps	Roast Chicken with Mediterranean Herb Stuffing & Tomato Basil Soup with a Touch of Cream	Garlic Spinach and Mushroom Sauté & Cod with Tomato and Capers
Tomato and Mozzarella Stuffed French Toast	Hearty Chickpea and Spinach Soup & Pork Loin with Mediterranean Herbs	Garlic Spinach and Mushroom Sauté & Cod with Tomato and Capers
Almond Butter Toast Delight	Turkish Meatballs in Tomato Sauce & Grilled Eggplant and Mozzarella Salad	Tomato and Basil Zucchini Noodles & Grilled Tilapia with Garlic Herb Marinade

Quick Berry Oat Crunch	Roasted Red Pepper and Feta Salad with Fresh Herbs & Balsamic Glazed Beef Steaks	Garlic Spinach Sauté & Baked Cod with Basil and Tomato Relish
Zucchini and Potato Frittata	Avocado and Quinoa Salad & Sumac-Spiced Pork Chops	Roasted Cauliflower with Tahini Sauce & Grilled Salmon with Olive and Caper Relish
Spinach and Feta Breakfast Wraps	Butternut Squash and Sage Soup & Za'atar Spiced Lamb Kebabs	Baked Garlic Parmesan Zucchini Chips & Citrus-Infused Grilled Shrimp
Banana and Walnut Oatmeal with Cinnamon	Mediterranean Fish Soup & Paprika-Rubbed Chicken Thighs	Asparagus and Lemon Risotto
Ricotta and Lemon Pancakes	Simple Greek Salad with Cucumber, Tomato, and Feta & Greek-Style Grilled Ribeye	Chargrilled Vegetables with Romesco Sauce & Cod with Tomato and Capers
Turkish Menemen (Tomato and Egg Scramble)	Roasted Red Pepper and Feta Salad with Fresh Herbs & Za'atar Spiced Lamb Kebabs	Shrimp Saganaki with Feta and Tomatoes & Garlic Spinach and Mushroom Sauté
Herbed Goat Cheese and Asparagus Frittata	Mediterranean Quinoa Salad with Bell Peppers and Olives & Garlic Butter Lamb Steaks	Baked Tilapia with Cherry Tomatoes and Olives & Garlic Spinach Sauté
Cretan Dakos	Greek Meatballs with Tzatziki	Baked Ratatouille with Crispy Chickpea Topping

SIMPLE TIPS FOR CREATING A BALANCED MEAL PLAN

Balance Nutrients: Include protein, carbs, and healthy fats in every meal.
Vary Ingredients: Rotate fruits, veggies, grains, and proteins for nutrition and variety.
Meal Prep: Batch-cook staples like grains and proteins to save time during the week.
Control Portions: Use measuring tools or visual cues for proper portion sizes.
Choose Whole Foods: Prioritize unprocessed foods like whole grains, lean proteins, and veggies.
Plan Snacks: Include healthy, pre-portioned snacks in your plan.
Stay Flexible: Adjust meals as needed for variety and convenience.
Hydrate: Include plenty of water or low-calorie drinks in your day.
Use Leftovers: Repurpose leftovers for lunches or dinners.
Keep It Simple: Stick to easy, time-friendly recipes to stay consistent.

Conclusion

Congratulations on embarking on this journey toward a healthier, more fulfilling lifestyle with the Mediterranean Diet! Through these 160+ simple and quick recipes, and over 2000 days of meal planning ideas, you now have a wealth of delicious options to help you nourish your body and enjoy food that supports your well-being.

The Mediterranean Diet isn't just a temporary way of eating; it's a sustainable, balanced lifestyle that emphasizes fresh, whole ingredients, mindful eating, and enjoyment of meals with family and friends. From the vibrant flavors of olive oil, fresh herbs, and vegetables, to the satisfying, protein-rich sources like fish, legumes, and lean meats, this diet is about celebrating food that fuels both your body and soul.

Remember, the key to long-term success lies in consistency. This cookbook was designed to make your daily cooking routine stress-free and enjoyable. Whether you're looking for quick weeknight meals, meal planning tips, or simply new ideas to keep your diet varied, you're equipped with the tools and recipes to create lasting, positive changes.

As you continue to explore and enjoy these recipes, feel free to adapt them to your taste preferences, experiment with ingredients, and most importantly—savor each bite. The Mediterranean way of eating is not about restriction, but rather a celebration of abundance, flavor, and nourishment.

Here's to many more years of health, vitality, and culinary enjoyment on your Mediterranean diet journey!

Made in the USA
Columbia, SC
07 December 2024

48648688R00057